P9-EJU-496

THE
NEW GUIDE
TO READING
AND STUDYING
THE BIBLE

THE NEW GUIDE TO READING AND STUDYING THE BIBLE

WILFRID HARRINGTON, O.P.

Introduction by Donald Senior, C.P.

Enlarged Edition

Michael Glazier, Inc.
Wilmington, Delaware

ABOUT THE AUTHOR

Wilfrid Harrington, O.P., is a distinguished author whose books have been translated into many languages. He is widely respected throughout the English-speaking world as a brilliant writer and lecturer on biblical topics. His books include *Mark*, volume 4 of *New Testament Message*, of which he is co-editor; and *The Prodigal Father: Approaching the God of Love*, volume 2 in the *Ways of Prayer* series.

First published in 1978 by Michael Glazier, Inc.
1723 Delaware Avenue, Wilmington, Delaware 19806

©1978 by Wilfrid Harrington, O.P.

Library of Congress Catalog Card Number: 78-55499
International Standard Book Number: 0-89453-092-5

Second Printing, 1979
Revised and enlarged edition, 1984

Printed in the United States of America

TABLE OF CONTENTS

INTRODUCTION 7

PREFACE TO REVISED EDITION 9

FOREWORD 11

GLOSSARY................................. 15

I. THE BIBLE

CHAPTER 1. What is the Bible? 23

CHAPTER 2. The Interpretation of Scripture 32

CHAPTER 3. Sampling the Word 42

II. THE NEW TESTAMENT

CHAPTER 4. The Books of the New Testament 51

CHAPTER 5. The Newness of the New Testament .. 103

CHAPTER 6. The Flavor of the New Testament 110

III. THE OLD TESTAMENT

CHAPTER 7. The Books of the Old Testament 145

CHAPTER 8. The Values of the Old Testament 158

CHAPTER 9. The Flavor of the Old Testament..... 162

IV. READING THE BIBLE

CHAPTER 10. The Bible as Story 201

CHAPTER 11. Why Read the Bible?............... 215

CHAPTER 12. How to Read the Bible 226

Introduction

One of the deepest joys of speaking about the Bible in a parish setting today is to see the spark of enthusiasm kindled in someone exposed to the beauty and power of the scriptures. But a persistent frustration is how to respond to these same people when they ask help in translating their initial enthusiasm into some serious reading of the Bible.

After reading *The New Guide to Reading and Studying the Bible* I expect my frustration level to go down. The next time someone interested in the Bible asks me where they can start, I will send them to this book. It is clear, informed, thoughtful. Best of all, it lives up to its title. It is, in fact, a guide to reading and studying what is a hauntingly beautiful but stubbornly difficult body of literature. The three questions which guide *The New Guide* are practical and to the point: 1) What is the Bible? 2) Why read the Bible? 3) How to read and study the Bible? Each question seems staggering, but the book does a remarkable job in giving good answers to all three. At the same time, the author is wise enough not to make this only a book *about* the Bible. Right from the beginning, the reader is invited to savor some biblical passages, to experience first hand the richness and diversity of the Old and New Testament. But even these first steps into an ancient yet strangely relevant world are guided by informed commentary on the background and meaning of the texts.

It is not surprising that a good and practical book like this should come from the pen of Wilfrid Harrington. He is a biblical scholar with unimpeachable credentials. But he is a scholar who also has the rare knack of making scholarship presentable for a general audience. Since 1963 he has written almost a book a year, including such works as *Explaining the Gospels* (1963), *A Key to the Parables* (1964), *Understanding the Apocalypse* (1969), *The Path of Biblical Theology* (1973), and his latest work, *Spirit of the Living God* (1977). As the titles themselves suggest, Fr. Harrington's works have been consistently marked by sound scholarship and pastoral sensitivity. The wisdom of a scholar and the gentle goodness of a pastor characterize as well the author's own personality. Saint Dominic, a man who believed that truth deserved to be preached, would be proud.

I am proud, too, and privileged to introduce this book.

Donald Senior, C.P.
Catholic Theological Union

Preface to Revised Edition

'This is the word of the Lord' the reader intones. 'Thanks be to God' we dutifully answer. Is there perhaps a lack of conviction, in the declaration and in the response? The scripture passage may not have been memorable at all. It may not have made much sense to us. Yet we suppose it must have some meaning, for it is 'word of God'. It is in the Bible, and we are urged to read and know our Bible. Is this a simple matter of buying a Bible and getting down to reading it?

No, it is not as simple as that. I have been studying and teaching the Bible for many years. I know that there is no easy way to understanding the Bible. I find myself more and more admiring the sophistication of the biblical writers. Many show remarkable literary skill; many were exceptionally gifted theologians. Their work has not only to be read. It must be studied. The Bible is a literary and theological treasurehouse. And it is word of God.

One who would enter the treasury, who would understand the word, needs a guide. This work is meant to be a guidebook. It begins by pointing out how writings of men can be word of God. Then, lest we drift into abstraction, we are asked to sample the New and the Old: to pause and read, not aimlessly, but to read carefully selected passages. This should give a feeling for the Bible. It could prove an exciting experience.

We look more closely at the New Testament: at the different writings, at what is special about it. A fuller study of certain areas is designed to alert one to the depth and subtlety of the writing and the sublimity of the message. The Old Testament meets with similar treatment: the books, the worth of it and its flavor. The final section faces the question, *Why read the Bible?* and goes on to offer advice on how to read it. It provides a select reading-list which lays bare the heart of the Old and the New.

The book had gone through two printings; a revision, rather than another reprint, seemed in order. Two new chapters (Two and Ten) have been added — on the interpretation of Scripture and on the Bible as story. Two other chapters (One and Four) have been largely rewritten. This revised edition, then, is notably fuller than the first and will, more effectively, aid the studious reading of the Bible.

To read and to study. There is no other way, there is no short-cut. It is a task that challenges our christian seriousness. To face the challenge and to persevere in the task is to enrich our christian lives. Then when we hear, 'This is the word of the Lord,' we can say our Amen with conviction and with thankfulness.

The thought of writing this book came from my friend Michael Glazier; its format grew out of discussion with him. I thank James J. Haley for his painstaking reading of my manuscript and for his helpful suggestions.

W.J.H.

Foreword

Before one faces up to the question: How to read and study the Bible? one should ask oneself: Why read the Bible? And this, in turn, invites the further basic question: What is the Bible? These three questions, each of them reasonable, all of them important, can very well form the program of this book.

I have said that the questions are not only reasonable but important because I believe that the Bible is important in itself and is important for me — and for you. You may well imagine that you know, perhaps know quite well, your Bible. That may be. But it might be that you have ideas about the Bible that are not quite right, that are not helpful at all. I have been, professionally, involved with Scripture, teaching Scripture and writing about it, for over twenty years. I write this book to help you to see the Bible in a new light, to help you understand it better, to appreciate it more. It might even, in some measure, enable this word of God to influence your life more positively and more deeply.

It may be, on the other hand, that you are not too familiar with the Bible at all. You may be aware that it has an importance, that you really ought to know more about it — but it remains strange and even foreign to you. You hear passages of Scripture read in church and you are genuinely puzzled. The readings are solemnly declared to be 'word of God' — and you wonder why God has to speak in such esoteric terms and why, often enough, the message is not particularly edifying? You are further assured that 'this is the word of the Lord' and you suppose that it must be so. But, to be honest, you may have your doubts. And the truth is that the Bible does not mean very much to you. And you seem to be able to manage very well without it.

It could be that the designation 'word of God' stands at the source of our puzzlement, or of our misunderstanding. One might, for starters, ask the question: if it is 'word of God' why is it couched in *human* language, in words of men? After all, God is God, and surely is capable of speaking to us directly — to the heart? Why, then, had he to speak in Hebrew and in Greek? Is it that Hebrew and Greek are his favorite languages and that he refuses to speak any other? And why should he have stopped speaking to us nearly 2,000 years ago? For if the Bible is 'word of God', as it is maintained to be, then God, it seems, stopped speaking to us at the last word of the New Testament.

There is another factor which you may not have thought of, but which should give you pause when you advert to it. We are Christians and the Bible is *our* Scripture. Look at your Bible however. You will find that the Old Testament runs to four-fifths of the whole. Now the Old Testament is, by definition, and by simple dating, earlier than Christ. In other words, the greater, the far greater, part of our christian Scripture is pre-christian. Does that not seem a little odd? And when you acknowledge the fact, and think about it, you will surely begin to realize that it cannot be all that easy to fit, comfortably, the pre-christian Scriptures into our 'christian way'. Perhaps you may have begun to appreciate why the Old Testament, in particular, does seem 'strange' to us.

You have regularly heard the Bible described as *the book* — even as 'the good book.' If you have ever tried to read the Bible you will have quickly come to realize that, apart from appearing between two covers, it hardly seems to be *a* book. It emerges as a collection of writings which, as one gets to know them better, display an impressive diversity, even within the Old Testament and within the New Testament. We have something more approaching a modest library than a book.

Why are the scriptural writings so diverse? Why is our Bible so predominantly Old Testament in extent? How, and in what way, is this varied literature word of God — and word of God for me? These are only a few of the questions we must consider in the framework of the three broad questions we have proposed at the beginning. It is hoped that the answers will not only be positive, but positively helpful, and that this *New Guide to Reading and Studying the Bible* will help you to hear the word of God in the words of men.

Glossary

It is hoped that reference to this glossary will spare the reader the chore of searching out in the text the meaning of a recurring term.

ALLEGORY — Allegory (where the details of a story have symbolic value as in The Wicked Vinedressers, (Mk 12:1-8) is extended metaphor and, as such, is a story that has both a literal and a metaphorical level. An allegorical story can well be a parable — as in the example cited. The customary sharp distinction between allegory and parable is invalid.

ANTHROPOMORPHISM — Speaking of God in human terms — God 'speaks', 'hears'; the 'hand of God'. We cannot avoid speaking of God in such terms.

APOCALYPSE — From a Greek word meaning 'revelation'. As a literary form an apocalypse is presented as a revelation, or a series of revelations, made to a seer by God or by an angel acting in his name. It culminates in God's final overthrow of evil and his vindication of the just. It is a crisis-literature. The great biblical apocalypses are the book of Daniel (more precisely Dn 7-12) and the Revelation of John.

APOCRYPHAL — The designation of writings purporting to be Scripture — but which are not. There are many apocryphal books related to both the Old Testament and the New Testament — of very unequal value and interest.

CANONICAL CRITICISM — An approach to the Bible which takes full account of its received or canonical form. E.g. Deuteronomy is read as the last book of the Torah rather than as an introduction to the Deuteronomical History.

CANONICITY — The canon of Scripture is the collection of writings recognized by the church as divinely inspired; canonicity is the character which the books acquire on being recognized by the church as inspired and normative.

CHRISTOLOGY — The theological understanding of the meaning and significance of Jesus. It especially concerns his relation to God: how and in what way he is Son of God.

CHURCH — Jesus gathered together a community, a family of God, a new people of God — later called Church. The Church is a preliminary stage, preparing for and already representing, the future Kingdom of God.

COVENANT — Originally a treaty graciously 'given' by an overlord. Yahweh gave a covenant to his people at Sinai: sealed and ratified in the blood of a sacrificial victim. Jeremiah spoke of a 'new convenant'. This new covenant with the new people of God was given by Jesus and sealed in his blood (cf 1 Cor 11:25).

DEUTERONOMISTS — A designation of the author(s) of the book of Deuteronomy and those imbued with its spirit. Their outlook was profoundly religious and striking in its singlemindedness: the nation stood or fell by its fidelity or unfaithfulness to Yahweh and to his Law.

DEUTERONOMICAL HISTORY — The books of Joshua, Judges, 1, 2 Samuel, 1, 2 Kings, with Deuteronomy as introduction. This complex material was edited by the 'deuteronomists' and bears the imprint of their theological outlook.

DIASPORA — 'Dispersion': The numerous Jewish communities 'dispersed' throughout the Greco-Roman world.

ESCHATOLOGICAL — Pertaining to the *eschata*, the 'last things'. Eschatology refers to the new age, the transformation of this world. But, with the coming of Jesus, this new age has already begun — we await the consummation. In the preaching of Jesus, for instance, the Kingdom of God is eschatological: the final intervention of God, his kingly reign, is (in Jesus) a present reality.

FORM CRITICISM (of the Gospels) — A method which studies and analyzes the form and structure of the gospel tradition. It identifies various types of traditional material (e.g. miracle-stories) and distinguishes the milieux (e.g. liturgy, mission, catechetics) in which the tradition was formed.

HELLENISM — From *hellēn* (Greek): The environment of Greek language and culture which pervaded the Mediterranean world after Alexander the Great. In the New Testament the hellenists are Greek-speaking Jews or converts from Judaism.

JUDAIZERS — Converts from (pharisaic) Judaism who maintained that full observance of the Mosaic Law was obligatory on Christians — even Gentile converts. Cf Acts 15:1; Gal 2:11-16.

KERYGMA — The 'heralding' or 'preaching' of the Good News: the missionary preaching of the Gospel to Jews and Gentiles.

KINGDOM OF GOD — More properly the 'reign' or 'kingly rule' of God. In Jewish expectation it meant God's definitive incursion into our history, marking the Last Age. What is new in Jesus' preaching is his declaration that the future kingdom is a reality here and now: present in him, in his works and words. Yet there is a tension between present reality and future consummation — the kingdom is now depicted as present, now as future.

MESSIAH — From a Hebrew word meaning 'anointed'. In Greek it is rendered *christos*, whence Christ. In Jewish expectation the Messiah would be God's instrument (*not* a divine figure) in ushering in his Kingdom. Jesus was something wholly unexpected: a Messiah who is Son of God.

MIDRASH — A Hebrew noun from the verb 'to search out'. It means a 'searching' of Scripture, an application of a text of Scripture to other times and circumstances. For instance, Dn 9:24-27 is a recasting of a text of Jeremiah (Jer 25:11-12). The qualification 'haggadic' means that the midrash is a freely composed narrative — a story.

PARABLE — A parable is a narrative having two levels of meaning. It has a specific religious or ethical purpose and is designed to challenge decision and invite action. The Good Samaritan (Lk 10:30-37), for instance, teaches that 'neighbor' is not defined by religion or race but by human need. And I am challenged to see my neighbor in the needy one and to be neighbor to him in turn.

PAROUSIA — The 'appearance' or coming of the glorified Christ at the end of salvation history. It is a dramatic way of expressing faith in a final act of God marking the goal of human history and the inauguration, in its fullness, of the Kingdom of God. Early Christians expected this consummation in their own time.

PENTATEUCH — Meaning 'five-fold' — the books Genesis, Exodus, Leviticus, Numbers and Deuteronomy: the first five books of our Bible.

PRIESTLY WRITERS — The editors (priests of the Jerusalem Temple) who gave its final form to the Pentateuch. The creation-story (Gen 1:1 - 2-4a) is a sample of their work.

PSEUDONYMOUS WRITINGS — Pseudonymity (the attribution of a writing, by the author, to another than himself) was a well-known and accepted literary convention in New Testament times. Thus 2 Peter is pseudonymous: the author, by identifying himself with Peter, shows that his intention is to transmit apostolic teaching.

REDACTION CRITICISM (of the Gospels) — A method which studies the contribution of an evangelist. It discerns between traditional material and the evangelist's modifications and additions. With the growing realization that the evangelist is a creative author, redaction criticism tends to become literary criticism and see a gospel passage as part of a carefully structured whole.

SCRIPTURAL INSPIRATION — The specific inspiration by the Spirit whose end-product is the Bible, and which makes it to be Word of God.

SIGNS — For John the miracles of Jesus are 'signs': mighty works performed in the sight of his disciples; the accent is on the communicatory value, the message, more than on the fact as such. Thus, the giving of sight to a blind man (Jn 9:1-12) is a sign of the spiritual light that Christ, who is Light, can give.

THEOCRACY — A society where God is recognized as the effective ruler. In the period of the monarchy, Judah was, in theory, a theocracy: the king was God's vicar. After the Babylonian Exile the Jewish state was a theocracy: the High Priest, God's vice-gerent, was its leader. The Kingdom of God would be the true theocracy.

TORAH — Commonly translated 'Law' — the Pentateuch is *the* Torah. Better rendered 'instruction', 'guide of life'. The Torah was regarded in Israel as a gracious gift of God. The attitude of later Judaism to the Torah led to legalism — the dictatorship of law.

TRADITION — Apostolic tradition is a vital link with the apostolic foundation-age of the Church. It is, in a real sense, the Church itself in its way of life.

TRUTH OF SCRIPTURE — Not *any* kind of truth but religious truth, saving truth. It is truth which pertains to our salvation. This truth is present in a variety of ways under different forms.

WORD OF GOD — The Bible is Word of God because its writers were inspired by the Spirit of God to produce this specific work. It is word of God in a way that no other word can claim. But it is word of God *in words of men* — the human dimension must be given its full weight.

YAHWIST — The conventional designation of the 10th century B.C. author of an important strand of the Pentateuch — of Genesis 2-4 for instance. So named because he applies the name 'Yahweh' to God from the beginning. See Gen 2:4 — in contrast to the 'God' of Genesis 1.

I
THE BIBLE

Chapter One

What Is The Bible?

A. Word of God

The Bible is word of God: this is admitted by all who take the Bible seriously. Yet, in practice, the designation — word of God — is misleading and has been, and is, the source of basic misunderstanding and has spawned a host of problems. For, if the Bible is 'Word of God' — what does that mean? Only humans can communicate *in words*. This being so, when one designates a divine communication 'word of God,' one is asserting that God does truly communicate with humankind. But not only so: one asserts that the form of communication is that most common form of converse among human beings, the form of human language. Revelation by word of God means divine revelation which has been given human expression by humans.

The implication is inescapable. Human words are time-conditioned; the same has to be so of the human words of Scripture. Does one thereby strip the Bible of its authority and challenge its uniqueness? Not at all. 'The fact that the "word" of the Bible is human and time-conditioned makes it no less "of God." In the Bible God communicates himself to the extraordinary extent that one can say that there is something "of God" in the words. All other words, patristic, theological and ecclesiastic, are words *about* God; only the

Bible is the word *of* God' (Raymond E. Brown, *The Critical Meaning of the Bible*, N.Y.: Paulist Press, 1981, p. 21). There is, however, one thing we need to be clear about and candidly acknowledge: one cannot *prove* that the Bible is word of God. That is a matter of *faith*. Its humanness is evident to commonsense.

Word and event

God has spoken to us in words, and through human spokesmen, because he has first and foremost spoken in and through our history. Yes: God's word to us has always primarily been in and through events; never has it been a matter of mere words. Israel came to know its God as the God who 'with a mighty hand and an outstretched arm' delivered his people from Egypt. Yet, word and event do blend. Scripture not only gives an account of events but offers, more importantly, an *interpretation of events*. Both together, event and interpretation, constitute revelation. For instance, a detailed description of the crucifixion of Jesus would depict only a brutal execution of a form common enough in the world of the time; the Christian interpretation of the event — the redemptive death of one who is the Son of God — makes all the difference.

The human word

If the Bible is, in large measure, the record of what God has done, it is also God speaking to us more directly: through or in the prayer-language of the psalmists, or in the language of wisdom of the sages. God has revealed himself, he has made himself known to men, he has taken the initiative, freely and lovingly. But his revelation is also invitation: he has made himself known not for his own sake but always 'for us men and for our salvation.' It is important to keep this in mind: God makes himself known for our sake. We must realize that what we come to know about God has, and is meant to have, a bearing on our lives. In this sense God's revelation of himself is wholly practical. Always, too, the God who has spoken to us is a God who has been understood by a *human* mind and who communicates with us in *human* language. To seek to bypass the human mediator of the Word is to ignore God's way of coming to us. It is to miss the human conditioning of God's word.

Full attention to God's intent and to the true nature of his word means that we will recognize and accept the relative contributions of each spokesman of God. No one of them has spoken the whole divine word, but each has heard, truly, in the realm of his concern, and according to his native capacity. The whole word is the word of the whole Bible, and not of any part of it. Some views and statements are incomplete. Some have to be not only filled out, but even corrected, by later discernment. All is word of God (in words of men), and always bears the stamp of the time and place of its utterance. This unavoidable human conditioning of the word is to be taken with the utmost seriousness. God's revelation has been given human expression. And no human word can speak the fulness of God.

B. Scriptural Inspiration

The Bible is regularly referred to not only as word of God but as inspired word of God. The tendency has been to think of 'inspiration' solely in terms of inspiration of Scripture. In truth, 'inspiration' is any movement of the Spirit of God; and, as a matter of fact, scriptural inspiration comes at the end of a process. Looking only to the Old Testament, we find that the action of the Spirit is indeed varied. In the first place, there is an inspirtion to act, that is, an efficacious

25

movement of the Spirit which takes hold of a man in order to make him perform certain deeds. Then there is, especially in the prophets, an inspiration to speak. The prophets are the interpreters of the Spirit and the effect of their inspiration is the proclamation of those 'Oracles of Yahweh' which teach and direct the people. 'Scriptural' inspiration takes care of the record of events, of forceful words of the prophets, of quieter words of the sages. Scriptural inspiration is not, by any means, the only action of the Spirit in the history of salvation. It is, though, a specific action of the Spirit that has led to *this* precise record of God's way with humankind and of the human reaction to God. The God who has communicated in events and in prophetic words and in words of wisdom now communicates in written words. Scripture is timeless word because it is word of God. It is time-conditioned word because it is mediated through human culture and human language. What matters is that it bears the stamp of the Spirit of God.

The Spirit of Christ

Scriptural inspiration means that the biblical writings originate with the Spirit of God and communicate the Spirit. In a more specifically christian sense scriptural inspiration means that the Bible is experienced by the faith-community as animated by the Spirit of Christ and as communicating the truth and power of the Holy Spirit. Nor is this a matter only of specifically christian writings (the New Testament). Already, the Old Testament had been acknowledged (in faith) by Israel as bearing the patent presence of the Spirit of God. Christians, conscious of the Old Testament's place in the life of Jesus and of the apostolic church, could recognize that the inspiring Spirit of Scripture as a whole was identical with the Spirit of Christ. It is this animation with the Spirit of Christ that gives Scripture its unique character. An important factor here is the role of those who receive the written word — the degree to which the church and the individual are able to recognize the Spirit in the writings he has inspired and to respond to him there.

Normativeness

In recognizing the inspiration of a biblical writing the church thereby acknowledges it to be *normative* for its life and practice. It cannot be otherwise. For, if Scripture, animated by the Spirit of Christ, is uniquely Word of God, it has, by that very fact, to be the last court of appeal for the christian community. As a further step, the church's recognition of the inspiration and normativeness of a book leads to the inclusion of the book in the *canon* of Scripture. The Greek term *kanon* meant originally a 'measuring rod' and then, in a derived sense, a 'rule' or 'norm.' The church Fathers used the word *canon* to designate Scripture as normative, as 'rule of faith.' Ultimately, the canon of Scripture came to mean what we understand by it today: the collection of divinely-inspired books recognized by the church as its *norma normans non normata* — the ultimate norm, the last court of appeal.

Canonicity

The history of the formation of the canon, the process by which the various books of both the Old Testament and the New came to be firmly accepted as word of God, is complicated. What seems to have happened is that those writings which eventually achieved canonical status had been *in practice* taken to be inspired and normative before ever there was any official decision in their regard. For instance, the bulk of the Old Testament was, by Christians, spontaneously regarded as word of God because it had been accepted as such by Jesus and by the christian community from the beginning. After all, the Spirit of Christ, which animates the Scriptures, would have guided the church in discerning that animation. And the discernment would have come, most naturally, through the community's life and practice.

'It is the act of canonization by the faith-community that makes the text canonical, an act which recognizes the text as inspired and normative, but which confers a third and separate character upon the text, viz., canonicity... The biblical books are canonical because the church has accepted them into the canon; the church has accepted them into the canon because she recognized them as inspired and normative' (p. 464) (Thomas A. Hoffman, S.J., C.B.Q., 44 (1982), 447-469).

Three factors, then, characterize the inspired writings: inspiration, normativeness, and canonicity. By way of summary, these separate and essential components may be described as follows:

Inspiration — animation with the Spirit of Christ, which is to say that a writing is experienced by the faith-community as communicating the power, truth and presence of the Holy Spirit.

Normativeness — means that the writing contains that which the church recognizes as normative for all time.

Canonicity — the decision of the church which recognizes the inspired and normative character of a writing and thereby makes it part of the christian Bible.

C. The Truth of Scripture

Is the Bible true? That really depends on what one means by the 'truth' of Scripture. One view is that 'the books of Scripture, firmly, faithfully and without error, teach that truth which God, for the sake of our salvation, wished to see confided to the sacred Scriptures' (Vatican II, *Dogmatic Constitution on Divine Revelation*, art. 11). And this is a wise approach for, indeed, the message of the Bible is emphatically religious and concerned with what pertains to salvation.

Yahweh is God

But here again the human aspect of the Bible comes into play. There obviously must be a development from the Old Testament on to the New. Even within the Testaments growth must be acknowledged and discerned. For instance, through the Exodus experience the Israelites came to know their God, Yahweh; but they knew him as just that: *their* God. Their religion was not yet, in our sense, monotheism. They did not deny the existence of other gods; simply, these gods were irrelevant. And their Yahweh was a 'jealous' God who would not tolerate their cult of any other god. In the course of time they came to understand that Yahweh was the Creator of all that is, that he is the only God. Thus we have the confident, indeed the triumphalist, monotheism of a Second Isaiah (Is 40-55) in the 6th century — though the 8th century prophets were already firm monotheists.

Does this imply that the 12th century Israelites (including Moses himself) were in error? Nothing of the sort. They had taken a firm, essential step, Yahweh was their only God: and therein is truth. Their understanding was not false: it was incomplete. It took time for experience and insight to grope towards the concept of the one true God. This is not the way of error; it is the way of humankind, of perception and of growth.

29

Jesus is Lord

To take an example from the New Testament: the development of christology (the theological understanding of Christ). We, as heirs of a sophisticated christology, can too easily forget that the first Christians had to grapple with their growing conviction that the risen Jesus belonged in the divine sphere, that he stood side by side with the only God. It could be no easy task to reconcile monotheism with the divinity of Jesus.

It seems that Christians quickly looked to the resurrection to find a key to the meaning of Jesus. Acts is formal and clear: God raised up Jesus and made him Lord and Christ (2:32-36); God, at the resurrection, exalted him as Leader and Savior (5:30-31); Jesus was begotten as God's Son through the resurrection (13:32-33). And there is the important pre-Pauline formula in Rom 1:3-4 — '. . . the gospel concerning his Son, who was descended from David according to the flesh and designated Son of God in power according to a Holy Spirit by resurrection from the dead.' Through human origin Jesus is son of David, while through resurrection, Holy Spirit, and power, Jesus is designated as uniquely God's Son. At this first significant stage of development the resurrection is regarded as the moment when Jesus' unique relationship to the Father was first grasped.

At a later stage we find in Mark a christology which involves the casting of the titles and the understanding of the risen Christ back to Jesus of Nazareth in the gospel account of his ministry and passion. In other words, it reflects the evangelist's understanding that the Lord Jesus Christ was Lord too throughout his ministry. Yet this is not enough. In the infancy gospels of Matthew and Luke the understanding of Jesus as Messiah, Son of David, savior, and Lord, is pushed back to the infancy period. It represents a stage in the

30

developing comprehension of him who is the christian Lord: he is Lord not only through resurrection, not only during his ministry, but also from the beginning of his earthly existence. From there the final step was the one to pre-existence and incarnation. This is achieved in John: 'In the beginning was the Word, and the Word was with God, and the Word was God ... And the Word became flesh...' (Jn 1:1,14).

Again we ask: was that first vague perception wrong —or only incomplete? Surely, the answer is obvious. It needed time for human minds to grasp the stupendous reality of the Incarnation. 'The truth, the whole truth, and nothing but the truth' is God's prerogative. Partial truth that is honest groping towards the full truth is thoroughly human truth. And the truth of the Bible, God's word in words of men, is *human*. It must be that the *whole* truth could not be formulated at the beginning — nor, for that matter, even at the end.

Chapter Two
The Interpretation Of Scripture

A slice of autobiography may, unexpectedly perhaps, be an effective way of illustrating how our understanding of Scripture has developed and changed very much over a remarkably short period of time. My formal theological course was completed in 1954 which (given a time-lag) meant that my biblical studies had been touched, to an extent, by the liberating encyclical *Divino affante Spiritu* of 1943. By the time I started on my teaching career (1957) the effect of that document had changed Roman Catholic biblical studies beyond recognition. Of course, even before 1943, the more receptive Catholic scholars had kept themselves fully in touch with developments in the scriptural world. They had, judiciously, assimilated contemporary biblical scholarship but were effectively muzzled by a Roman curia which was, on the whole, unsympathetic to such developments. Then, out of the blue, broke that dramatic document —authored, as is widely recognized, by the German Jesuit, Augustine Bea. The floodgates were down. The unprepared were taken by surprise. And, if unpreparedness brought upset the source of that should not be laid at the door of scholars. Had they been, earlier, granted their simple right to academic freedom, development would have followed a steady pace and not have come with a rush.

Vatican II

Before long, again unexpectedly, came the Second Vatican Council, which built on what had been achieved. By then Catholic biblical scholars had made an immense impact — a decisive impact as far as Vatican II itself was concerned. An objective assessment is always welcome and one may quote the verdict of a Presbyterian scholar. The whole of Chapter Ten of *New Directions in New Testament Study* by Patrick Henry (Philadelphia: Westminster, 1979, pp. 225-240) is a warm endorsement of recent Roman Catholic biblical scholarship. Henry concludes: 'The final two chapters (chapters 25 and 26) of the Constitution (*Dogmatic Constitution on Divine Revelation*) urge on all the Catholic faithful — clergy, members of religious orders, laity — the reading and study of the Bible. In a long historical perspective this is revolutionary. The Church in her late medieval times excommunicated, and occasionally burned, persons who undertook to provide the Bible in a language the laity could read for themselves. The Bible is a book that has demonstrated through the centuries a remarkable capacity to get things started, to make a difference in the way people think and act. When an authoritative Council of the Church directs the faithful — all seven hundred million of them — to get about the business of reading and studying the Bible, who knows what might happen?' (p. 240).

Gospel criticism

A glance at progress in the study of the synoptic gospels (i.e. Matthew, Mark, Luke) will give an indication of the developments referred to above. One notes, soon after World War I, the emergence of *form-criticism*. What this means is that one got behind the text of a gospel to identify, if one could, the stuff that went into its shaping. Even our earliest gospel

(Mark) did not originate at an evangelist's desk. First there was Jesus himself, his teaching and his deeds, and the Christ-event of his death and resurrection. Then came the preaching: stories about Jesus, collections of his parables, summaries of his words. Form-criticism looked not only to the forms but also to the reasons for those forms. For instance, it seems quite sensible to assume that the passion-narrative took shape in a liturgical setting, as background to the celebration of the Eucharist.

Next was the turn of *redaction-criticism* — which is little more than a fancy way of acknowledging that an evangelist (let us say, Mark) had more than a little to do with the gospel attributed to him. At first the concern was to separate out the recognizable editorial retouches and insertions of an evangelist from the traditional material he had used. It was felt that the former would point to his distinctive theological concerns. More recently, especially in the United States, it has been recognized that the choice of traditional material and its deployment are essential features of an author's concern and contribution. In short, the common-sense view has prevailed that an evangelist is the *author* of his gospel; he has put his stamp on the whole of it. It is acknowledged, too, that an evangelist has written out of a given community and for a given community. The concern of Luke is not that of Mark; more precisely, each stresses different areas of christian concern. Realisation of this fact goes a long way towards understanding the reason for notable differences between gospels. Mark and Luke have not been named indiscriminately. It is highly likely that Luke, in composing his gospel, made wide use of Mark and the manner in which he has used his source is eloquent. The tendency, then, has been to look to the *author*. If one can discern his intention one is on the way to grasping the meaning of his text.

34

The text

The latest trend in biblical interpretation is to concentrate on the *text*. In other words, it is recognized that biblical criticism is, necessarily, literary criticism — the Bible *is* literature. A form of modern literary criticism is structuralism. This approach looks to the rules of language and concentrates on the 'deep structures' of language which every author has to respect. Some structuralists have maintained that a literary text is wholly independent of its author. The element of truth is that when an author launches his text he loses authority over that text — all the more obviously when an author is no longer around to comment on any interpretation of his text. The biblical writers have been dead for some considerable time.

The realisation that a text has a life of its own does not justify arbitrary interpretation — a text cannot be made to say just anything one may wish it to say. In this connection the contention that a text is quite independent of its author (as though it mattered not at all who wrote it) is surely misguided. Any given writing has an historical setting and is culturally conditioned. What is true is that a text — and we are dealing with classic texts — may have a meaning beyond that which the author willed, a meaning, or meanings, perceived by the reader. We should be clear that one is not speaking of arbitrary meanings but of meanings which the text can sustain.

Commonsense

After more than twenty years of teaching one becomes increasingly aware of the importance of commonsense. I had appreciated the value of investigating tradition behind a biblical text (form-criticism) and the practical implications of taking seriously the fact that a text has an author (author-criticism). Today I am aware that, in a reasonable concern to discover the intention of an author (but can we hope to pin down the intent of an ancient writer?) we had tended to neglect the one tangible factor: the text. For it has to be admitted that preoccupation with tradition and author did tend to get in the way of the text.

The text, after all, is paramount. This does not mean, we have urged, that we make what we like of it. It does mean that we strive to listen to the *message* of the text. It means that we be alert to the revolutionary and explosive quality of biblical texts. In practice, we have tended to 'tame' the Bible. It is surely perverse to reduce sayings of the prophets and of Jesus to conventional wisdom — but that is just what we had done. Already we have admitted that a text may have meanings beyond the first meaning of its author. But whenever that meaning has Jesus or Paul or the prophets mouth platitudes we can be sure that the 'meaning' is misunderstood. We need to assume that any true meaning of Scripture will be challenge; not always dramatic, but rarely banal.

Canonical interpretation

Another recent concern is a way of looking at Scripture which, on the one hand, is not new at all while, on the other hand, it follows on the trends we have noted above. If it is sensible to assume that a given writing is a meaningful whole, it is reasonable to assume that a traditional grouping of writings may have purpose. For instance, the Torah (or Pentateuch) has, in Jewish and Christian tradition, always been taken as a unity; Deuteronomy, then, is, traditionally, part of the Torah. On the other hand, historical and literary analysis has shown that Deuteronomy is unquestionably related to the subsequent books: Joshua — Judges — Samuel — Kings — the so-called Deuteronomical History. Deuteronomy, and notably its earlier chapters (chs 1-3), is the introduction to this History. Yet, in the Bible, the book is given to us as the last will and testament of Moses, rounding off the saga which begins in Exodus. One is not called on to repudiate the valuable results of deuteronomic studies; one is asked to recognize the biblical setting of Deuteronomy.

Similarly, one could argue that Genesis 1-11, a product of the Jerusalem Priestly school, is, in its present form, quite late (5th-4th century B.C.) and one might feel that the passage should be studied in that late setting. The fact remains, however, that, as Scripture, the passage is given to us as the prologue to the Pentateuch (for that matter, as the prologue of the whole Bible). And quite rightly, because the theological and anthropological contribution of these chapters (what they teach us about God and humankind) make them, indeed, a fitting introduction to the Bible. To pursue the point: it is undeniable that these same chapters are made up of two easily recognizable traditions, one from the 10th century B.C. and the other very much later (see Chapter Nine). Yet, the end-product is a new text with its own message.

What all this amounts to is that we have come (or come back to) regarding the *Bible* as a literary and theological artifact. Its structure is not haphazard. This is especially true of the threefold division of the Jewish Bible. The *Torah* ('instruction') binds together the books Genesis-Exodus-Leviticus-Numbers-Deuteronomy. As we have pointed out, despite the legitimate scholarly attachment of Deuteronomy to the subsequent History, one may not ignore the canonical status of the book as the final part of the Torah.

The designation of the second major division of the Hebrew Scriptures is an eye-opener: 'The Prophets' — Joshua-Judges-Samuel-Kings forming the 'former prophets.' Medieval Christians had tagged these same books as 'historical' and had thereby created for themselves and us a host of (pseudo) problems. One is not suggesting that Joshua — Kings are unhistorical. One urges that history (in our sense) is not the intent of the editor of these traditions. Presented as it is by the deuteronomical theologian the story carries a powerful religious message. Perhaps 'message' is the key. The word of the Bible is not primarily an account of things past nor an utopian vision of things to come. It is, basically, a challenge to the hearers of the word. To many demands of Scripture could be appended the explicit word at the close of the parable of *The Good Samaritan* (Lk 10:30-37): 'Go and do likewise' (10:37).

The third division of the Hebrew Scriptures witnesses to the commonsense we have commended. It is *kethubim* —The Writings. There is a designation elastic enough to accommodate any writing and it hospitably houses such disparate works as Job, Song of Songs, and Esther. Somehow, that elusive title reminds us that we should be sensitive to the native character of the biblical writings. It is wise to take them on their own terms.

Scripture in church

In our look at the interpretation of Scripture we have effectively stressed the importance of the Bible. The implication might be that we Christians are 'people of the book,' that our religion is based on a sacred book. Christians have sometimes given that impression. When, however, we look to Old Testament times and to the New Testament age we find another situation. What we come to see is that both the Old and the New grew out of the life and experience of a people. In both cases the people, not the book, came first. And the book must ever find its setting in the ongoing life of a people. Only in the midst of a believing people does the Bible come alive. A fully christian reading of Scripture is 'in Church' — in the context of a living community.

Scripture and tradition

Tradition, understood precisely as apostolic tradition, a link with the apostolic foundation-age of the christian Church, is something active and living. Its function is to transmit the 'apostolic preaching' which includes everything needed for living the christian life, as well as for the growth of the christian faith. What is handed on is not merely a doctrine but an entire way of life. It is the Church itself in everything that it is as well as in everything that it believes — its teaching, life, and liturgy — which is the full embodiment of tradition. What the process of tradition perpetuates is the Church itself.

Tradition makes the word of God progressively pervade the total life of the Church. It gives the Church a living understanding of the scriptures. The words of the Bible must become living and effective in the Church; when tradition is brought to bear on the written word, it becomes alive and relevant. Tradition serves scripture. It is firm in sustaining the essential understanding of scripture which the Church has held from the time of the apostles. It prudently embraces the valid insights of scholars which deepen that understanding. And tradition is free and flexible enough in its expression to be able to draw out, with divine authority, contemporary answers from the letter of scripture. Through the joint action of tradition and scripture God speaks here and now to his Church, and the gospel becomes a living voice rather than a historical record.

The New Testament, composed in large part of occasional writings (written on particular occasions and for specific purposes) does not claim to represent the total content of the faith of the early Church. Nevertheless we may reasonably assume that the writings of the New Testament, being the permanent and divinely-willed norm for the Church of later ages, do contain all the essential truths of the christian faith. Then we must remember that dogmatically-binding declarations of the Church are such only because they are connected with truths which have been revealed by God for *our salvation*. This means that the whole ministry of the word is under scripture. The teaching office of the Church which can make these binding dogmatic declarations, must know that scripture, read by it with the assistance of the Spirit, tells it what is right. Scripture remains the last court of appeal for theology and for the Church.

The teaching office

Vatican II has made clear that since it is a christian authority the teaching office of the Church will take the form of service rather than dominance. It is the servant of the word of God. The teaching office can only teach what it has received through scripture and tradition. It must first listen to the word, and then preserve and expound what it hears. It can only bind the faithful to believe on divine faith what it has itself heard in the deposit of faith. Thus, a teaching is already believed by the Church at large before the teaching office makes it a dogma that must be believed by everyone. Dogma gives precision to the understanding, expression and communication of the faith within the christian community. As such it is imposed under obligation by those who hold authority in the community. But they can only oblige us to believe what they have already heard of the word of God.

The Bible

Ours is not a religion of the book — but the book matters mightily. This advertence to the role of scripture in guiding and shaping the dogmatic declarations of the Church underlines our insistence on the place the Bible ought to have in the life of every Christian. But we have the more serious intent of insisting that the Bible is attached to life. We read it, first and foremost, because we *are* Christians. We study it, not as a message of the past but as word of God *to us*. And it is such because of its accepted place in the life of the christian people. It is word of the living God to a living people of God.

Chapter Three

Sampling The Word

There is little point in talking about the Bible without direct reference to the Bible. It is time to get down to brass tacks. To read about the Bible makes sense only if we already have some idea of what it is. There is only one way to get to know the Bible: to read it. The trouble is, reading the Bible is not as simple as it sounds. It is, in fact, easier to say how *not* to read the Bible. One should not pick up one's Bible and open it at the first page with the intention of working through to the end. That of course, is our normal practice when we take up a book we mean to read. But, as we have said, the Bible is not really *a* book but a collection of books, a modest library indeed. And many of the individual writings show different strands or strata which may well confuse at first. Nothing is better calculated to put the aspiring Bible-reader off for life than a dogged attempt to read the Bible straight through.

How, then, is one to set about it? I suggest that first we *sample* the writings — turning to some books or sections that are more readable, understandable and congenial. It will not be difficult to compile a short list. One will find, perhaps somewhat to one's surprise, that the Bible can be enjoyable reading. One will then have the incentive to read more — but this further reading will also need to be directed. At that stage the object of the selection will be to lead to the heart of the Scriptures.

A. Which Bible?

There is an obvious prerequisite: a version of the Bible. Happily, several can be recommended. There is the *Revised Standard Version*. This text is excellent for study purposes because, without being over-literal, it keeps closely to the original, and avoids paraphrase. But it does not have notes and sets out the text in chapters without any attempt to indicate the logical divisions or to point out different strands as they may occur. One should take care that one's copy of the RSV contains the Apocrypha — the books Sirach, Wisdom, 1 and 2 Maccabees, Tobit, Judith, Baruch, and parts of Daniel and Esther. These are accepted as Scripture by the Roman Catholic and Orthodox Churches, but not by the Protestant Churches. A simple way of making sure that you have them is by getting the RSV Catholic Edition. Or, better, *The Oxford Annotated Bible with the Apocrypha* which does have introductions to the writings and helpful notes.

Chapter and verse

We have mentioned 'chapters' above, and this is as good a place as any to advert to the fact that the division into chapter and verse, which we take for granted, is quite late and is somewhat haphazard. The original writings had no such divisions: each book appeared as a block. In the Middle Ages, it was found that reference, especially to the longer writings, could be impractical. It is not very helpful to be told, for instance, that such and such a verse occurs in the gospel of Matthew — it could be quite a chore to track it down. So, the text was broken into sections, labelled 'chapters'. On the whole this was reasonably well done. Yet, it not infrequently happens that a chapter does not represent a logical unit. Only when Bibles began to be printed was the verse-division introduced: again simply to help in locating a text. It is so much easier to find, say, Matthew 6:2 than to dig for the same text in 'Matthew'.

The Jerusalem Bible has splendid introductions to the books and quite extensive notes. And it sets out the text with generous and helpful sub-divisions. These features, and especially the format, appeal to one who is trying to get to know the Bible. On the other hand it is far from being a great translation. Happily this situation is being redeemed. An entirely new version, based on the latest revised edition of the *Bible de Jérusalem*, is near completion and should be out in 1983. This means, too, that the notes are updated. The new JB is likely to be the aspiring reader's best choice.

The New American Bible is in straightforward and pleasant English — naturally with an American flavor. The introductions and notes are brief yet informative. It can be warmly recommended. The *New English Bible* is, perhaps, the best modern version in English, but it has the shortcoming of the RSV: giving only the plain text arranged in the traditional chapter divisions. But, here too, the Oxford Study Edition of the NEB has introductions and notes. *Today's English Version*, while leaning more toward paraphrase than any of the others, is faithful and reads well. The reader can rest assured that, with any of these versions, he can come to grips with the word of God. He had better fight shy of *The Living Bible* which is, avowedly, a paraphrase and which regularly imposes a particular theological interpretation on the text — rather than letting it speak for itself. The same goes for other paraphrases of the Bible.

B. Sampling The New Testament

It is not particularly helpful to browse through the New Testament. But it is beneficial to glance through it purposefully, reading selected passages. Here we offer a sample — but not a random sample. The reader who will have paused to read these passages (and that is the whole purpose of the sample) will be in a better position to profit from our following chapters. So, do now take up your *Bible* and read.

1. *Philemon.* This is a typical letter, short and to the point; we feel at home with this sort of writing. Notice the solicitude of Paul for this runaway slave and his courteous approach to Philemon.
2. *James, chs 1-2.* Practical advice marked by a rare commonsense view of things.
3. *Acts, chs 27-28.* The famous shipwreck journey of Paul — a fine piece of descriptive writing.
4. *Luke, ch 15.* The 'parables of mercy'. Notice that in the parable of The Prodigal Son there are *two* sons. Might we have something of that elder son's impatience with God's mercy to the sinner?
5. *Mark, chs 14-16.* The Passion according to Mark.
6. *Matthew, chs 5-7.* The Sermon on the Mount. Matthew has made a compilation of sayings of Jesus. There is no real logical sequence. Do not be surprised to find some of the sayings obscure.
7. *John, ch 9.* This blind man is an attractive character. For John the miracle shows Jesus to be the one who gives spiritual light and sight.

8. *John, ch 15.* A passage to be read meditatively. In it the risen Lord speaks directly to me.

9. *1 Corinthians, ch 13.* Paul's famous 'hymn to love'. His understanding of love as practical concern is inspired by the example of Jesus.

In conjunction with this passage read Matthew 25:31-46. Do not worry about the 'judgment-seat' factor, but do worry about the disturbing fact that the 'sheep' are as surprised as the 'goats'. In being kind to their fellows they were showing kindness to Christ — though they had not been conscious of that.

That will do for our short list. It should convey something of the variety of the New Testament. We have teaching of Jesus in parables and sayings, Paul at his most simple and most profound, the down-to-earth James, the descriptive writing of John and of Luke (author of Acts), and Mark's moving story of the Passion. A taste, no more. But, at least, we are no longer talking about some vague entity called the 'New Testament'.

C. Sampling The Old Testament

In some ways it is easier to make a sample selection of the Old Testament. But given the extent of the Old Testament, it will be a modest taste indeed.

1. *Tobit.* Surprisingly 'modern' — a true novelette. Notice how skillfully the stories of Tobit and of Sarah are blended in ch. 3. And the book closes in familiar 'they lived happily ever after' fashion.

2. *2 Samuel, chs 11-12.* The moving story of the sin and repentance of David. The whole of 2 Samuel is

remarkably vivid — the finest piece of narrative writing in the Old Testament.

3. *Genesis, chs 42-45.* The reunion of Joseph with his family in Egypt. Notice how Joseph declares that God had directed the whole affair.

4. *Hosea, chs 6 and 11.* So much for that touchy, stern 'God of the Old Testament'!

5. *Jeremiah, ch 20:7-18.* A prophet's cry from the heart.
   ch. 31. The same prophet's words of comfort to a shattered people.

6. *Song of Songs, chs 4-5.* The ecstasy of love. True love of man and woman is a gift of God.

7. *Job, 38:1-40:5.* With splendid irony the Lord questions Job. He did not have an answer to his personal problem — what does he know of *all* the works of God? Man stands before his Creator.

8. *Sirach, 25:13-26:18.* About women good and bad. A good example of an ambivalent view of woman. The biblical writers were men of their time.

9. *Psalm 23.* 'The Lord is my shepherd' — a prayer of confidence.
   Psalm 51. A prayer of repentance.
   Psalm 104. Hymn to God the Creator.

One should have little difficulty in appreciating the story of Tobit and the narratives about Joseph and David. Hosea and Jeremiah introduce us to a pair of prophets and their God. There is the magnificent poetry of Job and the lyrical poetry of the Song. Sirach gives a display of flattery and cynicism in his attitude to women. And the prayers and hymn give a glimpse of the Psalter.

Our sampling of the Word should make what we must do more definite. And the reader may begin to feel that, to an extent, it is possible to have 'Scripture without tears'.

II

The New Testament

Chapter Four

The Books of the New Testament

The reader will have noticed that in our sample readings we put the New Testament first. This was done deliberately because it may be taken for granted that the reader is more familiar with the New Testament and it is only good sense to begin with the better known. Similarly , in this fuller treatment, we take the New Testament first, and for the same reason. Our decision is a purely practical one. When we have outlined the contents of the New Testament we shall seek to indicate what is specifically new about it. And then, with a closer look at some areas, it is hoped to convey something of its flavor.

A. The Gospels

A gospel is a new kind of literary form. There is nothing quite like it outside of the New Testament. The later apocryphal gospels, works for the most part of christian piety, are pale reflections of the real thing (the term 'apocryphal' means that they are not Scripture). Our gospels are a mixture of narrative and discourse, centered on the person, life and teaching of Jesus of Nazareth, with special emphasis on his death and resurrection. He is the focus; he gives meaning to all. Yet, as we have come to realize, all is shot through with the light of the resurrection. For the gospels are documents that are at once historical and religious — and there ought not to be a division between 'fact' and 'interpretation.' Indeed, interpretation is necessary if an occurrence, what happens, is to have meaning and impact. And the interest and meaning which an event bore for those who were conscious of it as event and felt its impact becomes part of the event, becomes historical in its turn. The evangelists presented the 'facts' with the intention of bringing out the meaning which the events had for those who encountered them. They set out to voice the faith of the early Church. The nucleus of that faith was that the crucified Jesus had risen from the dead.

John has told us, with all desirable clarity, the aim of an evangelist. He has no intention of giving us an account of the life and times of Jesus of Nazareth. His selective account of the 'signs' of Jesus was written that the christian disciple may go on believing that the historical figure, Jesus, is the Messiah of Jewish expectation, that he is Son of God. He wrote that, through their faith in Jesus, Christians may find life in him (cf Jn 20:31). The gospels are proclamations of the Good News, not records destined for an archive. If they do seem to concern themselves with what Jesus of Nazareth had done and said, they are aimed at christian communities striving to live the christian way.

A gospel is written for *believers*: it is a christian document addressed to Christians. More specifically, each of our gospels was, in the first place, written for a determined christian community and with the needs of that community firmly in mind. But, inspired by the Holy Spirit, they continue to speak, across the centuries, to christian communities of all time.

1) THE PERSON BEHIND THE GOSPELS

The New Testament is all about a person whose role in history has been remembered. The starting point for an account of the mission of Jesus is his encounter with John the Baptist: the call which Jesus experienced when he was baptized by John. Jesus was conscious of being authorized to communicate God's revelation because God had made himself known to him as Father. His 'Abba' as a form of address to God expressed the mystery of the mission of Jesus. At the baptism he understood his mission as Messiah, Son of God and Servant of the Lord, in the power of the Spirit. It was the acceptance of his vocation.

The Ministry

According to the general run of the gospel narratives Jesus, during the first part of his ministry, was engaged in three main types of activity.

1. He was engaged upon a broad appeal to the public. His aim was to make people aware of the presence of God as an urgent reality and to invite their appropriate response.
2. He set himself to minister to human need by healing the sick in body and mind, by awakening faith in those who had lost hope. And he sought to lead people into a new life under the inspiration of a personal attachment to himself. By thus going about doing good, he gave concrete form to his message of ultimate salvation.
3. While his outward vocation took the form of a teacher of religion and morals, his whole outlook and approach differentiated him from rabbinic Judaism. He challenged the people to rethink their ideas and hopes, only to be branded a blasphemer. He censured

his contemporaries for casting aside God's warnings. Thus, in his mission, controversy was forced upon him.

Death and resurrection

In the faith of the Church the passion was not the end but the goal and crown of the earthly activity of Jesus. When all the evidence is taken into account (and the eucharistic words are the most important allusions to Jesus' suffering) it is clear that Jesus expected and announced his suffering and death. Many would hold that Jesus had found the answer to the necessity of his suffering and death in scripture, especially in Isaiah 53, the Song of the Suffering Servant of the Lord.

Because the disciples did not experience it as an event in history but rather as belonging to the last age, Christ's rising from the dead is presented as a resurrection to glory rather than as a return to earthly life. Whereas the crucifixion is clearly an historical event, a happening in time, the resurrection is an event beyond time (beyond death) and belongs to another order. In this sense it is not 'historical,' in the same way that the crucifixion is. It belongs to the new age and is thus 'eschatological.' The resurrection is utterly real, but it belongs to another order.

The Person

Let us look briefly at this Person as the disciples met him and we meet him now. Firstly, Jesus was conscious of himself as the bringer of salvation: hence his testimony to himself is part of the good news which he preached. This is why the empathic 'I' permeates the entire tradition of his sayings. A study of the language and style of Jesus in his sayings, especially in the parables, shows how clearly his personal characteristics stand out. In their simplicity, their closeness

54

to life through masterful, short description, and their Semitic cast, the sayings point back to Jesus himself.

The character of Jesus is discerned not only in these sayings but in his every action. His loving understanding of 'the poor' and his new attitude towards women and children mark an incursion of the new Kingdom of God into old social standards. He accepted women as disciples because he expected all his disciples to control their desires. With his 'unless you become as little children' he brought children closer than adults to God. His whole ethical approach was concerned with the dignity and responsibility of each human being before God. He taught 'with authority,' respecting the freedom of the person. It was an authority resting not on any official status or prestige, but on some indefinable quality in Jesus.

The Message

Though Jesus was conscious of being a prophet and bearer of the Spirit, he did not simply take his place in the sequence of the Old Testament messengers of God. He was *the* last messenger. Through him God was speaking his final word. Jesus came with a proclamation, and the central theme of his message was the kingly reign of God. The really new element in Jesus' preaching of this kingdom is that here and now its consummation is dawning. And the heart of Jesus' message can be found in a promise, the first beatitude: 'Blessed are the poor!' In promising to these, the poor and the heavy-laden, the reign of God, Jesus was making his most radical reversal of the standards of the time which held that all those who were disreputable or ignorant (such as precisely Jesus' own followers) were barred from access to salvation. Yes, here was an extraordinary new message: salvation was destined only for 'beggars' and 'sinners.'

Repentance

Jesus uttered a call to repentance and gave the assurance of forgiveness. Repentance is for Jesus less conversion than an unconditional trust in the Father. It is learning to say Abba again, like a child. That is why, paradoxical as it may seem, that repentance is joy. Jesus' call to repentance reached beyond individuals to a whole people of God. Jesus' mercy was especially expressed in the forgiveness of sins. The divine forgiveness which the new community of his follow-ers has experienced is the motive for their own unlimited capacity to forgive one another.

The Church

Jesus sought to gather together a community of salvation. In a wealth of pictures he constantly spoke of the new people of God he was gathering together. The new people of God stood in contrast to other 'remnant' groups — Pharisaic and Essene groups, even the disciples of the Baptist — because of one decisive element: a keen awareness of the boundlessness of God's grace. They were sure of this through poignant personal experience: the disciples, formally installed as the new people of God at the Last Supper, so soon deserted their Master. Yet, Jesus' forgiveness re-created them. They knew that, as the first members of the Church, they owed their position to the magnanimity of their ill-used Master.

Incarnation

Only after the resurrection did the disciples truly begin to understand who Jesus really was, to grasp the significance of his person, his life, and his teaching. The theologians of the early Church began to articulate the relation of Jesus of Nazareth to God. Christology, our understanding of the person and mission of Christ, cannot remain abstract, but must be concerned with the events and meaning of Jesus' life. The fact of the incarnation is fundamental.

The incarnation involves the poignant fact of paradox or scandal, this mystery of Jesus as both God and man. The Word-made-flesh is the offence: the revealer comes as a man who cannot prove to the world his claim to be son of God. The offense must be overcome by accepting Jesus in faith. The bold grandeur of the Son of Man is that, while he is still the afflicted one identified with everyman, the earthly person with 'nowhere to lay his head' and about to suffer, he is also the same Son of Man to be seated at God's right hand. The paradox of the incarnate Christ, the life-giver, is that he must tread the earthly road of distress to conquer that distress. He must assume human life to deliver humanity. And he must suffer in order to be raised from suffering into glory. The enduring 'scandal' of Christianity is that the total otherness which alone can save man is God as he has revealed himself historically in the man Jesus.

The Cross

The cross is at the heart of the New Testament. Though sin and anguish and death are still in the world, the problem of guilt has been solved by the cross. The sinner finds gracious forgiveness. Paul understands his ministry through his own personal, humanly painful experiences, and for him preaching meant 'the word of the cross.' By experiencing the dying of Christ, the apostle communicated Christ's life to the community through the effects of his preaching. The cross is not the end, and there is in the New Testament a necessary emphasis on the resurrection. The resurrection may be seen as a new revelation in the history of God's word: it is 'God's interpretation of the cross.'

Holy Spirit

There is a special fruit of the resurrection-ascension: Jesus' sending of the Holy Spirit. In John's gospel the Spirit comes to complete Christ's presence rather than to supply for his absence. Jesus promised the Spirit because he had much to say that his disciples could not yet have comprehended (cf Jn 16:12). To confess that Jesus has come in the flesh is to receive the Spirit of truth. For Paul the presence of salvation is manifest in the fact that the risen Christ is present, through his Spirit, in his community, and rules the life of the Christian. The New Testament theologians — the Synoptists, Paul, John, and the others — all build their Christologies on this message: that God's salvation is found in Jesus of Nazareth, the carpenter and teacher whom God had made Messiah. Throughout its pages the New Testament concerns itself with the truth that he who comes is not only victor and savior but also the person familiar from the gospel record of his earthly life of humility and suffering.

2) MARK

What is now recognized as the earliest of our gospels — Mark — was long written off as no more than an abridged version of Matthew. Today it is clear that this gospel stands firmly on its own merits. And we acknowledge that Mark is a far more skillful writer than had commonly been conceded.

The gospel of Mark is built up of two complementary parts. The first (1:14 - 8:30) is concerned with the mystery of Jesus' identity; it is dominated by the question, 'Who is Jesus?' The emphasis in this first part of Mark is on Jesus' miracles, while the little teaching that is contained in it is addressed to the crowds, and is largely parabolic. The second part (8:31 - 16:8) is concerned with the messianic destiny of Jesus: a way of suffering and death. The emphasis in this second half of Mark is on Jesus' teaching, which, now directed to his disciples, builds upon their recognition of him as Messiah, and is concerned mainly with the nature of his messiahship and with the suffering it will entail both for himself and his followers.

Plan of Mark

PART I. *The Mystery of the Messiah:* Revelation of Jesus' Person 1:14—8:30.

Three sections, each *beginning* with a summary of the activity of Jesus and a narrative concerning the disciples and *concluding* with the adoption of an attitude in regard to Jesus.

A. Jesus and the Crowds 1:14—3:6 [1:14f, 16-20; 3:6]
B. Jesus and His Own   3:7—6:6a [3:7-12, 13-19; 6:1-6a]
C. Jesus, the Disciples and the Gentiles
              6:6b—8:30 [6:6b, 6:7-31; 8:27-30]

CONCLUSION AND TRANSITION   8:27—33
    Confession of Peter
    First Prophecy of the Passion
    Correction of Peter

PART II. *The Mystery of the Son of Man:* Revelation of Jesus' Sufferings 8:31—16:8
A. The Way of the Son of Man   8:31—10:52
    Signposted by three announcements of the fate of the Son of Man and three instructions on the lot of the disciples.
B. Jesus in Jerusalem   11:1—13:37
C. Passion and Resurrection 14:1—16:8
    The Later Ending   16:9—20.

The Christ

Already the central passage, or hinge, of Mark's gospel (8:27-33) raises the crucial question. We find that the passage is concerned not primarily with an historical episode in the ministry of Jesus (Peter's confession at Caesarea Philippi) but with a situation of the church for which Mark is writing. Historically, Jesus and Peter engage in dialog. At a deeper level 'Jesus' is the Lord addressing his Church and 'Peter' represents fallible believers who confess correctly , but then interpret their confession incorrectly. Mark is thinking of his community, he is concerned about its understanding of Christ. The confession of Peter is the facile profession of too many of Mark's contemporaries: 'You are their Christ.' Everything depends on what they mean by that confession and its influence on their lives. They cannot have a risen Lord without a suffering Messiah; they cannot be disciples without walking his road of suffering.

Jesus is the Messiah; of that Mark is sure — but he is a disconcerting Messiah. The question stands, writ large: Who, then, is this? That Jesus would have permitted himself to be taken by his enemies, to be maltreated and mocked by them, to be put to death by them, is something that the contemporaries of Jesus and the readers of Mark could scarcely comprehend. Yet, if one has not come to terms with this 'scandal' one has not grasped the originality of Jesus, in particular, the Jesus portrayed by Mark. Jesus did not come as judge with sentence and punishment for those who will not receive the gift of forgiveness and salvation he offered to them. He came as the one who will let himself be crushed by the intent of those who resist him and who would be rid of him.

In the long run, what is incomprehensible is the suffering and death of the promised Messiah who would bring in the kingdom of God, of the Son of God who would reveal the Father. The originality of Jesus flows from the contrast between his heavenly authority and power and the humiliation of his crucifixion. Mark's 'messianic secret' is designed to reconcile two theological affirmations: Jesus, from the first, was indeed Messiah — and yet had to receive from the Father, through the abasement of the cross, his title of Messiah. The meaning of his life is that, as Son of God, sent by the Father, he had come to deliver humankind from all its enemies, from foes within and from foes without. He came to forgive sins not to chastise sinners. He came, but he will not impose. When it came to the test, rather than force the heart of man, he humbles himself and allows himself to be taken and shamed and put to death.

Suffering

'The Son of man must suffer many things' — the messianic story is no uninterrupted success story: it is a story of suffering, rejection, failure. This fact must color all we say about life and salvation. Jesus immediately runs into opposition: 'Peter ... began to rebuke him.' Quite obviously, Peter has spoken for all of us. Jesus confirms this: 'You are on the side of men' — you think the thoughts of man. Not the thoughts of the arrogant, the proud, but the natural reaction of those who shrink from a way of suffering. Have we, at bottom, any different idea of salvation from that of Peter? Can we really conceive salvation other than in categories of victory? We experience the saying of Jesus again and again as contradiction, we cannot reconcile ourselves to it. The rebuke of Jesus did not change Peter: he will deny the suffering Messiah. The other disciples will sleep and will abandon him. And the Church, which began with the disciples who failed to understand will, time and again, like them, fail to understand.

Victory

What is the meaning of the word that follows the prediction of suffering and death: '...and after three days rise again'? These words are not meant to allay our fears, not meant to soften the stark reality of suffering and death. That word of the victory of the Son of man over death is a promise of victory for the oppressed, the vanquished, the silent in death

— the forgotten. It is a word of warning against our human way of exalting the victorious and the triumphant. Through the suffering Messiah victory is possessed by the vanquished; through the dead Messiah life is possessed by the dead. He and his way are the sole guarantee of our victory and of our life.

Discipleship

Christians may be children of God but they are really such only on condition that they understand what it means, and live with its demands. Mark's own understanding of discipleship is the same as Paul's: 'if children, then heirs, heirs of God and fellow heirs with Christ, provided we suffer with him in order that we may also be glorified with him' (Rom. 8:17). His preoccupation with discipleship follows hard on his concern with Christology. The way of discipleship has been firmly traced by Jesus himself: 'If any man would come after me, let him deny himself and take up his cross and follow me' (8:34). For Mark, there is no other way of discipleship than that. The Christian shares in the victory of Christ, but no more than Jesus is he preserved from suffering and death. He must walk the same road that Jesus walked (10:30; cf 8:34-38).

If Mark has presented his Christology in terms of the life of Jesus, he has presented his teaching on discipleship in terms of the disciples of Jesus. They are painted in their fragile humanness. Here, again, is something close to the realism of Paul. It is not only in Galatians and in the letters to the Corinthians that we encounter Christians with more failings than virtue; the 'moral' part of each of Paul's letters plainly envisages frail and fickle men and women. 'The disciples' are a reflex of Mark's community. They are caricatures, starkly drawn, as Mark through them stresses the vital importance of coming to know Jesus and bluntly states his conviction that without the cross there is no hope at all of knowing the Lord. It is this concern that accounts for the unbelievable obtuseness of Peter and the rest. All disciples of the Lord should have the honesty to see themselves in these disciples. They had been called by Jesus and had responded to his call. He bore with them, in loving patience. They had failed him, but he had remained true. And Mark closes on a note of quiet confidence as the disciples, on the other side of cross and resurrection, wait for a meeting with the Lord in the 'Galilee' of their hope. Not all had failed: the silent, steadfast women had remained faithful to the end (15.40—16:8). Perhaps a lesson of Mark, yet to be learned, is that the community of Christ will come of age when the dignity of woman and her place in his church are acknowledged not only in word but in truth.

3) MATTHEW

The gospel of Matthew falls naturally into seven parts — with the first part, the Infancy Gospel, forming a prologue.

	Plan of Matthew	
I.	Prologue: Infancy Narrative	1-2
II.	The Kingdom Appears	
	The Preliminary Manifestation	3-4
	Sermon on the Mount	5-7
III.	Jesus' Saving Mission	
	Ten Miracles	8-9
	Missionary Discourse	10
IV.	The Hidden Kingdom	
	Opposition and Division	11-12
	Parables of the Kingdom	13
V.	The Kingdom Develops	
	Formation of the Disciples	14-17
	Community Discourse	18
VI.	Towards the Passion	
	Mounting Opposition of Judaism	19-22
	Judgment Pronounced	23-25
VII.	Passion and Resurrection	26-28

The structure of chapters 3-25 is precise: five sections, each containing a narrative part and a discourse. Each of the discourses has a brief introduction (5:1-2, 10:1-5; 13:1-3, 18:1-2; 24:1-3) and each is closed by a stereotyped formula (7:28; 11:1; 13:53; 19:1; 26:1). These five central parts of Matthew are not so many disconnected units; there is a close link between them. The narratives indicate the progressive movement of events, while the discourses illustrate a parallel progress in the messianic concept of the kingdom of heaven.

The Great Commission (28:16-20)

In the dramatic conclusion of the gospel, the glorious Son of Man, in the apt setting of a 'mountain,' a place of revelation, commissions his Church. We are rather taken aback to read (v. 17) that, of the eleven disciples, 'some doubted.' Matthew is drawing for his community a picture of every Christian community — believers caught between adoration and doubt. Jesus solemnly declares that through his death-resurrection he has been given, by the Father, total power over the universe (v. 18). He is, therefore, in a position to launch a universal mission. During his ministry Jesus limited his concern to Israel (10:5-6; 15:24); in the new era the good news is for all. Consequently, he duly commissions his representatives and sends them into the world to make disciples of 'all nations.' It is important to be clear that this solemn commission, so theologically important, is *not* historically a command of Jesus to his Church at its beginning: Acts 1-15 and Gal. 2 show that the reception of Gentiles and the mission to them were bitterly resisted. This commission reflects the experience of a Church that had become open to all, a Church tranquilly convinced that it had become what the Lord had meant it to be.

One becomes a disciple through baptism in the name of

the Father, Son and Holy Spirit — a trinitarian formula from the baptismal liturgy of Matthew's Church. Disciples must be taught *Jesus'* commands. Christians do not live by the ten commandments — even though, of course, Jesus' teaching includes much of what was in the Mosaic Law. For the Christian, Jesus' word is the ultimate law of morality; in that word will he discern the will of God.

Finally, we have Jesus' great promise of v. 20b: 'Lo, I am with you always, to the close of the age (the end of time)' —Matthew has skilfully rounded off his gospel by catching up the God-with-us (1:23) of his prologue. Matthew does not speak of a 'departure' or of a 'farewell' of Jesus. Rather, he places the community at the heart of the universal power of the resurrection. The 'end of time' which he has in mind designates the time of the Church (cf. 13:39-40; 24:3). It corresponds to the 'hereafter' of 26:64, where Jesus tells Caiaphas, 'hereafter you will see the Son of Man seated at the right hand of Power...' Jesus is promising his help as God himself, echoing all his assurances throughout the gospels: 'Fear not!; 'I am with you!'; 'It is *I*!' Whereas Luke closes with a farewell blessing and ascension (Lk. 24:51) here in Matthew Jesus assures us that he will be abidingly present in the congregation. Moreover, what is present is not his static presence in one chosen group, but his dynamic and helping presence for a worldwide mission.

Thus, Mt. 28:18-20 both assigns to Jesus the functions of Yahweh in the Old Testament and sums up Matthew's view of the *Kyrios* in the New. He has universal lordship, he gives commands that determine the whole life of God's people and their relationship to him and he promises to be the sustaining Lord at all times. Will he not keep his word? 'Where two or three are gathered in my name, there am I in the midst of them' (18:20).

Community

In the first discourse, the Sermon on the Mount, Matthew presents Jesus as Messiah in word (chapters 5-7). The purpose of the narrative section which follows (chapters 8-9) is to propose Jesus as Messiah in deed, because this section is entirely made up of miracle stories. Then follows the Missionary Discourse addressed to the Twelve (chapter 10) which is succeeded by another narrative section beginning with the question raised by John the Baptist, 'Are you he who is to come, or shall we look for another?' (11:3). The evangelist manifestly expects his readers to ask themselves the same question. But Matthew believed that a decision regarding Jesus necessarily involved a decision concerning his Church. An authentic commitment to Jesus was possible only within the context of membership in his community.

Church

In this gospel it becomes exceedingly difficult to distinguish between the disciples and the Community (or Church) because in Matthew's eyes they blend into one. This is evident in the instructions given to the disciples in Mt 18. It is here that Matthew brings together his significant ideas on the Church: true greatness in the Kingdom (vv. 1-4), scandal (5-10), the Lost Sheep (12-14), brotherly care and correction, authority in the Church (15-18), association in prayer (19-20), and forgiving offences (21-35). The Church is a family of children of the Father. Jesus is present in the midst of his Church — an idea framed by the Immanuel promise of 1:23 and the promise to be 'with us always' in 28:20. We find he is with his followers, present in his missionaries (10:40), in all in need (25:35-45), in all received in his name (18:5), and in the assembly . When the disciples are persecuted it is because they represent Jesus and imitate also his sufferings. Matthew too sees the community as a ship beaten by the waves, as he shows in the story of the stilling of the storm (8:23-27). In Matthew this episode becomes a paradigm of discipleship for, even more than in Mark, his boat becomes a 'ship of the Church;' and the cry 'Save, Lord' is at once a prayer and a confession of discipleship.

Kingdom

Matthew's church is seen in the perspective of the coming judgment, and the task of discipleship is interpreted accord ingly The seven Kingdom-of-God parables (chapter 13) combine both ecclesial and eschatological motifs — 'eschatological,' pertaining to the last age, the End. Jesus rules over the Church, and from the Church over the world — thus realizing the Kingship of God in the present period of salvation. The Church is the link between accomplishment here and now and final consummation. The members of the Community are the personal members of the Church who have submitted to God's rule in Jesus. They keep it warm and alive as persons, rather than as an institution. In short, the Church is a preliminary stage and school preparing for and already representing the future *basileia* or Kingdom.

4) LUKE

Luke was a second-generation Christian who wrote about 80-85 A.D. Though a Gentile convert (for such, it seems, he was), he was concerned with Israel and acknowledged clearly the place of Israel in God's salvation-history. He did not look to an imminent parousia; his two-volume work (Gospel and Acts) was written for Christians who lived in the post-apostolic age. 'Today,' 'now' is the time of salvation; *now* life is poured out in the Holy Spirit. But now, too, is the period of *ecclesia pressa*, a church under stress. Luke has shown what may be made of Jesus' deeds and words in a time after the era of Jesus. For us of the twentieth century, conscious of a gap of two millennia between the first proclamation of the christian message and our own striving to assimilate that message, Luke's form of the kerygma may be more congenial than others.

To appreciate Luke's purpose and achievement, his second work too, that is, *Acts of the Apostles*, must be taken into account. Then one can see that his object is to present the definitive phase of God's saving plan, from the birth of the Baptist to the proclaiming of the gospel in the capital of the Gentile world — Rome. Acts is not, in the first place, a history of the church; its first concern is the spread of the Word of God. Luke's theme is the progress of the Good News from Jerusalem to Rome. His is a message of salvation to the Gentiles. Simeon had seen in Jesus 'a light for revelation to the Gentiles' (Lk 2:32) and Paul's last words to the Roman Jews are: 'Let it be known to you then that the salvation of God has been sent to the Gentiles: they will listen' (Acts 28:28).

If concern is with Good News to the Gentiles the beginning of the gospel attests that the Church does not replace Israel but that, himself come from Judaism, Jesus strives, with the help of the Holy Spirit, to *renew* Israel. The salvation which he proclaims and achieves means that one is brought to God. He found that the marginalized — Galileans, women, 'sinners' — were more open to his challenge than the Judeans and their leaders. But his offer was to all, for Israel needed saving as much as the Gentiles.

In the Gospel, after his account of the infancies of John and of Jesus, Luke turns to the preaching of the kingdom of God in Palestine first by the precursor and then by the Messiah. At the close of his work he has Paul proclaiming the kingdom at the centre of the Roman world (Acts 28:30-

31). The Gospel tells of the mission of Jesus and of the saving events of his death and resurrection; it ends with his glorification at the ascension. Jesus had come as the Messiah of his people and had found himself rejected by them. But his mission had not failed. He had brought salvation (Lk 24:47).

Salvation History

Luke is the theologian of salvation history — the entrance of salvation into history. He alludes to a fundamental divine 'plan' for the salvation of humankind, one which was being realized in the activity of Jesus (7:30). The idea of such a plan is what underlies the necessity (e.g. 'was it not necessary that the Christ should suffer these things and enter into his glory,' 24:26) which is often associated with what Jesus does or says and with what happens as the fulfilment of Scripture. That the plan of God concerns the 'salvation' of humankind receives a special emphasis in the Lucan writings. Luke alone among the synoptics gives Jesus the title 'Saviour' (2:11).

Salvation had come with Jesus. After the ascension, men and women would be saved through him and because of what he had accomplished. The events of the life of Jesus were decisive for the world, constituting the beginning of the last days. For Luke, too, Jesus was the fulfilment of all the promises, and that in spite of the outward circumstances of his life which blinded the eyes of his contemporaries to the reality before them. This implied that all that went before Jesus was preparatory. Yet, preparation, fulfilment in Christ, and eventual universal salvation through him in these last days, together form one divine plan for the salvation of the world, a plan progressively realized through history.

For Luke salvation history has three phases: a) Period of Israel, from creation to the appearance of John the Baptist: the time of the law and the prophets (1:5-3:1); b) Period of Jesus, from the baptism of John to the ascension of Jesus: the time of Jesus' ministry, death and exaltation (3:2 - 24:51); c) Period of the Church: the time of the spread of the word of God (Lk 24:52 — Acts 28:31). If the creation is the beginning and if the spread of the word will persist to the close of time, then Luke's understanding of salvation history is emphatically universalist. The new inbreaking of divine saving activity into human history includes the extension of salvation to persons outside of God's chosen people of old. The change involves a distinctive view of Israel. God has not replaced his chosen people of old with a new one. The church is not a new Israel but a reconstituted Israel with Gentiles taking their place beside Jews who had accepted the message of Jesus. No other biblical writing underlines with the same vigour the common vocation of Jew and Gentile.

Christology

Lucan christology must be fitted into the pattern of Luke's salvation history. One starts with the *absence* of the risen Lord. A comparison of the conclusion of Matthew's gospel with that of Luke alerts one to the remarkable theological pluralism of the early church — and underlines the perversity of the sustained attempt in recent times at one 'official' theology. In Matthew, the risen Lord declares: 'Lo, I am with you always, to the close of the age' (Mt 28:20). The Lucan Jesus departs this world until the parousia (Lk 24:44-53; Acts 1:9-11); for Luke, the risen Messiah of Israel is no longer with his people on earth. At his ascension, Jesus had left his disciples, has taken his place at the right hand of God. This fact leaves Luke free to concentrate on the man of

70

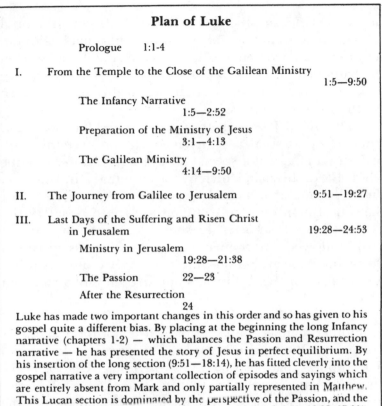

Plan of Luke

Prologue   1:1-4

I.   From the Temple to the Close of the Galilean Ministry
                                                                    1:5—9:50

       The Infancy Narrative
                1:5—2:52

       Preparation of the Ministry of Jesus
                3:1—4:13

       The Galilean Ministry
                4:14—9:50

II.   The Journey from Galilee to Jerusalem   9:51—19:27

III.   Last Days of the Suffering and Risen Christ
       in Jerusalem   19:28—24:53

       Ministry in Jerusalem
                19:28—21:38

       The Passion   22—23

       After the Resurrection
                24

Luke has made two important changes in this order and so has given to his gospel quite a different bias. By placing at the beginning the long Infancy narrative (chapters 1-2) — which balances the Passion and Resurrection narrative — he has presented the story of Jesus in perfect equilibrium. By his insertion of the long section (9:51—18:14), he has fitted cleverly into the gospel narrative a very important collection of episodes and sayings which are entirely absent from Mark and only partially represented in Matthew. This Lucan section is dominated by the perspective of the Passion, and the journey to Jerusalem is seen as a journey to death (cf. 9:51; 13:22; 17:11). Thus, despite the general agreement with Mark and Matthew, the third gospel has a distinctive character.

Nazareth who walked among us. We, who are so tempted to short-circuit the incarnation, would be well advised to concentrate on Mark and Luke. If John it is who has given us the notion of incarnation, it is Mark and Luke who stress for us the humanness of the Son.

For Luke, Jesus is the eschatological prophet — a prophet who is also the wise man of Israelite tradition. As

71

prophet it is not surprising that Jesus (like Jeremiah) should face misunderstanding and opposition, nor that he should, in the end, meet violent death. Jesus does not die, a hero, on the battlefield. He dies, faithful prophet, a martyr's death. Luke is intrigued by Jesus, fascinated by this man's concern for the poor, the outcast.

The life of Jesus has its own thrust and forms a unity. Luke refuses to single out any one event, not even the death of Jesus, and give it a special saving significance. It is the whole life of this man which by the faith that it inspires and the 'following' that it challenges, played a saving role: 'For the son of man came to seek and to save the lost' (19:10). Consistently, after Easter, Luke focuses on the struggles of Jesus' followers. His sequel to the story of Jesus is not cast in the realm of the marvellous but in the reality, often painful, of the christian Way. There is nothing triumphalist about Luke.

For Luke, the word of God was made flesh in Jesus but in another manner than for John. It is not the Johannine pre-existent Word but the word of God formerly addressed to the prophets that has taken flesh in Jesus (Acts 10:36-37). One may equally well say that in Jesus the flesh becomes word: the messenger becomes the message. In their turn the apostles carry on the incarnation of the word as they become the human and suffering bearers of God's message. They carry the word differently from Jesus — in his name, not in their own.

The christological titles are the sign of the non-conformity of Jesus. In his *life*, Jesus is conformed to the prophets of Israel. By the *titles* bestowed on him he stands radically apart from them. The incarnation of the word in his life has a specificity which the presence of God in the prophets and apostles does not carry. Thus the infancy gospel, far from being an appendage to Lucan christology, is where the lines of that christology come together. On this point, Luke is close to John. The theology of Luke is christological: it is linked to Easter and Ascension, because of the Passion — but also because of the Nativity. (See F. Bovon, *Luc le Théologien*, Neuchatel-Paris 1978, pp. 206-210).

Soteriology

Luke has told the Jesus-story not only with christological but with soteriological intent: what Jesus did, said, and suffered had and has a significance for and bearing on human history. Acts 4:12 makes this clear: 'There is salvation in no one else, for there is no other name under heaven given among humankind by which we must be saved.' It had been argued that Luke has downplayed 'the Cross.' The fact is that reference to the death of Jesus in the Lucan writings is impressive. Luke does not seek to suppress the tragedy and mystery of the cross nor undervalue its saving role. He does not question the need for the disciple of Jesus to deny himself, to take up the Cross and follow the Master.

Then there is the way in which Luke sees the effects of the Christ-event. 'Salvation' is clearly an important effect. What he means by it is best summed-up in a saying of Jesus himself: 'The son of man came to seek and to save the lost' (19:10). While the verbal form 'to forgive sins' is frequent in the Synoptics, the abstract form 'forgiveness of sins' is a Lucan usage. Luke sums up Jesus' work as the release of men and women from their debts (sins) in the sight of God. By all that he was and all that he did he has cancelled the debt incurred by their sinful conduct. In the sayings of Jesus 'peace' stands for the bounty that he brings to humankind. And if he seems to deny that his coming brings peace (12:51) it is because he knows that men and women will have to make a decision about him, either for him or against him.

Those who accept him into their lives will know that peace which he alone can bring.

5) JOHN

When one turns, from any of the Synoptic Gospels, to the Fourth Gospel, one feels oneself in a different world. There is, in the first place, a marked difference of language. Gone is the simple, vivid language of the synoptic Jesus; the Johannine Jesus speaks a markedly 'theological' language. The subject matter, too, of John's words of Jesus reveals their uniqueness. The Johannine Jesus is the bringer of a revelation which apparently retains little contact with the proclamation of the kingdom of God on the lips of the Jesus of the Synoptics. What the Johannine Jesus reveals, constantly and exclusively, is himself.

In the mind of the fourth evangelist the earthly Jesus merges with the risen and glorified Lord. He is aware of his divine origin. He speaks in full consciousness of his unity

---

Plan of John

THE PROLOGUE (1:1-18)

An early christian hymn, probably stemming from Johannine circles, which has been adapted to serve as an overture to the Gospel narrative of the career of the incarnate Word.

THE BOOK OF SIGNS (1:19 — 12:50)

The public ministry of Jesus where in sign and word he shows himself to his own people as the revelation of his Father, only to be rejected.

Part One:	The Opening Days of the Revelation of Jesus	1:19—51+ 2:1-11
Part Two:	From Cana to Cana — various responses in Jesus' ministry in the different sections of Palestine	2—4

74

Part Three:	Jesus and the principal feasts of the Jews	4:46—10:42
	4:46-54	*Introduction*
A.	5:1-47	*The Sabbath* — Jesus performs works that only God can do on the sabbath.
B.	6:1-71	*Passover* — Jesus gives bread replacing the Exodus.
C.	7:1-8:59	*Tabernacles* — Jesus replaces the water and light ceremonies.
	9:1-10:21	Aftermath of Tabernacles.
D.	10:22-39	*Dedication* — Jesus the Messiah and Son of God is consecrated in place of the temple altar.
	10:40-42	Apparent conclusion to the public ministry.
Part Four:		Jesus moves towards the hour of death and glory 11-12
A.	11:1-54	Jesus gives men life; men condemn Jesus to death.
	11:55-57	Transition.
B.	12:1-36	Scenes preparatory to Passover and death.
		Conclusion: Evaluation and summation of Jesus' ministry. 12:37-50

75

THE BOOK OF GLORY 13-20

To those who accept him Jesus shows his glory by returning to the Father in 'the hour' of his crucifixion, resurrection and ascension. Fully glorified, he communicates the Spirit of life.

Part One:		The Last Supper	13-17
A.	13:1-30	The Meal	
B.	13:31—17:26	The Last Discourse	
	Division 1:	The departure of Jesus and the future of the disciples.	
	Division II:	The life of the disciples and their encounter with the world after Jesus' departure.	
	Division III:	The concluding prayer of Jesus.	

Part Two:		The Passion Narrative 18-19	
A.	18:1-27	The Arrest and Interrogation of Jesus.	
B.	18:28—19:16a	The Trial of Jesus before Pilate.	
C.	19:16b-42	The Execution of Jesus on the Cross and His Burial.	

Part Three:		The Risen Jesus	20:1-29
A.	20:1-18	At the Tomb.	
B.	20:19-29	Where the Disciples are Gathered.	
	Conclusion:	A Statement of the Author's Purpose.	20:30-31

THE EPILOGUE 21.

An added series of post-resurrection appearances in Galilee.

A.	21:1-14	The Risen Jesus Appears to the disciples at the Sea of Tiberias.
B.	21:15-23	The Risen Jesus speaks to Peter.
C.	21:24-25	The (Second) Conclusion.

with the Father. Yet, in the discourses, John wishes Jesus to be heard — not himself. In the Synoptics, too, tradition was permeated by and interpreted in the light of faith. In John this process has reached its climax so that the fourth gospel is a presentation completely dominated by the vision of faith.

Double expression

A notable feature of John is the frequent use of double or ambiguous expressions. Such expressions, when spoken by Jesus, are first understood by his interlocutors in the obvious or natural sense, and he then goes on to explain the further, the real meaning. For example, in 2:19, the 'temple' of which Jesus speaks is not the building — as the Jews believed — but the temple of his body (2:21). More characteristic are such words as the adverb *anothen* (3:3,7) which means 'again' (and was so understood by Nicodemus) and also 'from above' (the meaning intended by Jesus). In 3:14 we read of the Son of man being 'lifted up.' The same expression occurs in 8:28 and 12:32-33; in the latter case a note makes it clear that crucifixion is meant. The evangelist regards the 'elevation' of Christ on the cross as a symbol of his 'elevation' to heaven through resurrection and ascension. In John's eyes, the death, resurrection, and exaltation of Christ are all aspects of one and the same mystery; hence, he can regard the exaltation on the cross and the exaltation to glory as one movement.

The Movement of Thought

In the narrative matter, the structure of the gospel as a whole displays a notably dramatic element. This skilfulness of presentation is also present in the longer individual episodes, such as the Samaritan woman, the cure of the blind

77

man, the raising of Lazarus. In these episodes the reader is brought stage by stage to the full self-revelation of Jesus. And the reader, too, comes to an increasing certainty of his faith. The longer narrative complexes illustrate the conflicts of opinion, the antagonism between belief and unbelief. At the same time, these episodes serve to present the great struggle between light and darkness, a struggle in which, seen from the outside, the powers of darkness and unbelief appear to be gaining the upper hand. Even in the shorter passages such as the marriage at Cana, the cleansing of the temple, and the healing of the official's son, dramatic presentation is not lacking. Here, too, one finds the moment of suspense before the liberating vision of faith.

An aspect of the dramatic in John is present in the emphasis placed on 'signs'; the signs are mighty works, performed in the sight of Jesus' disciples, miracles. Still, it is by contrasting 'miracle' and 'sign' that we can best understand John's intention. The restoring of sight to a blind man is a sign of the spiritual light that Christ, who is Light, can give, because he viewed such actions of Jesus as pointers to a deeper, spiritual truth. We are not always left to work out these hidden meanings for ourselves, because, in many cases, they are brought out in the discourses that accompany the signs; we are also thereby provided with a criterion for judging other passages where such comment is lacking. The signs are closely linked to the work of Jesus on earth; the purpose is to bring out the deeper dimension of his works, to reveal the glory of the Incarnate One.

Nowhere does the difference between John and the synoptic gospels strike one more forcefully than in the discourses of Jesus: the discourses of the fourth gospel are quite distinctive. John does not reason in our western manner: he testifies, he affirms. He does not set out to prove a thesis by building up consecutive arguments until the conclusion is reached. Instead, his thought moves around a central point. Jn 14:1-24 can be taken as an example of how the thought 'circles,' repeating and insisting, while, at the same time, moving forward and upward to a higher level. Again, one may instance the two great 'parabolic discourses' in John —the Shepherd and the flock (10:1-18) and the Vine and the branches (15:1-10). Both passages are built on similar lines: first a presentation of the matter, the 'parable' (10:1-5; 15:1-2), followed by the strictly Johannine development: a method of concentric thinking which progresses in new circles. It is a meditative way of thought which, instead of proceeding by arguments delves deeper into its subject to gain a deeper and higher understanding of it. This distinctive Johannine movement of thought seems to have no direct parallels. It is a personal style, achieved by meditation on the revelation of Jesus Christ and used to clarify this revelation.

The Passion Narrative

The Passion narrative of the Fourth Gospel (chs 18-19) splendidly illustrates the distinctiveness of that Gospel. John presents the Passion as the triumph of the Son of God. The *dramatis personae* are sharply characterized. Despite appearances, *Jesus* is always in control. He is the Judge who judges his judge (Pilate) and his accusers ('the Jews'). He is the King who reigns, with the cross for a throne — 'I, when I am lifted up from the earth, will draw all to myself.' *The Jews* are not the whole Jewish people but its leaders who see Jesus as a danger to them, the Establishment, and who are determined to destroy him. *Pilate* recognizes, and three times acknowledges, the innocence of Jesus. He desperately tries to compromise but ends by yielding to political blackmail. He is a man who will not make a decision for or against Jesus —and finds himself trapped.

Jesus before Pilate (18:28 — 19:16). The synoptic accounts of the trial before Pilate tell us little whereas John's dramatic reconstruction does bring out the significance of it. Only John makes clear why Jesus was brought to Pilate in the first place and why Pilate gave in to have him crucified. Only John shows the interplay of subtle (and not so subtle) political forces on Pilate and indicates how Pilate's original questioning of Jesus concerned a political charge against him. Yet Mark, we now realize, has given the key to the trial in the title 'King of the Jews' (15:2); thereafter he stresses that it is as King of the Jews (messiah) that Jesus is rejected by the crowd and crucified.

There is a theological reason for John's stress on the Roman trial. We are to see Pilate in the light of the rest of the Fourth Gospel. He provides an example of an attitude to Jesus which is neither faith nor rejection: the typical attitude of those who try to maintain a middle position in an all-or-nothing situation. Pilate's refusal to make a decision for or against the Light leads to tragedy. Because Pilate will not face the challenge of deciding for the Truth in Jesus and against the Jews, he thinks he can persuade the Jews to accept a solution that will make it unnecessary for him to declare for Jesus. This is the Johannine view of the episodes of Barabbas, the scourging, and the delivery of Jesus to the Jews as 'your King.' For John, this trial is our own tragic history of temporizing and indecision. Pilate, the would-be neutral man is frustrated by the pressure of others. He failed to listen to the truth and decide in its favour. He, and all who would follow him, inevitably end up enslaved to this world.

Pilate yields to the Jewish demand for Jesus' crucifixion (19:12-16). John's account of the passing of sentence of death is detailed, dramatic and theological; the only points of parallel with the synoptists are in the repeated cry for crucifixion and the outcome of Jesus' being 'handed over.' The

Old Testament background to this verb used by all the evangelists implies that Jesus was 'delivered up' by 'the definite plan and foreknowledge of God' (Acts 2:23). The real trial is over when the Jews utter the fateful words, 'We have no king but Caesar!' This is akin to the statement in Matthew's account: 'His blood be upon us and upon our children' (Mt 27:25). Both evangelists are reflecting not history but apologetic theology. The tragedy of Jesus' death was viewed through the hostility between Church and Synagogue in the late first century A.D. The audience at the trial are made to voice a christian interpretation of salvation history.

John also tells us that it was noon on Passover Eve when the fatal renunciation of the Messiah was voiced. This was the hour when the Passover lambs were being sacrificed in the Temple. It is supreme Johannine irony: the Jews renounce the covenant at the very moment when the priests begin to prepare for the feast which annnually recalled God's deliverance of his covenanted people. By the blood of a lamb in Egypt Yahweh had marked them off to be spared as his own. Now, they know no king but the emperor and they slay another Lamb. At this moment, just before the Passover, as Jesus set out for Golgotha to shed his saving blood, the trial of Jesus ends with the fulfilment of that proclamation at the beginning of the gospel: 'Behold the lamb of God who takes away the sin of the world' (1:29).

The last word of Jesus — 'It is fulfilled!' (v.30) — is a cry of victory: now Jesus will draw all to himself. 'He gave up his spirit': Jesus dies, but his Spirit will take over his work of drawing mankind to himself. Jesus is now glorified in the completion of his 'hour,' the fulfilment of God's purpose —and so the Spirit now is given (cf 7:39).

The final episode, the breaking Jesus' legs and the flow of blood and water (31-37) is the only part of John's crucifix-

81

ion narrative which has no parallel in the synoptics. The flow of blood and water is another prophetic reference to the giving of the Spirit. On a secondary level this flow symbolizes the sacraments of Eucharist and Baptism and points to their source in Jesus; through these sacraments the life of Jesus is communicated to the Christian. Blood and water flow from the *dead* Jesus. The drama of the cross does not end in death but in a flow of life that comes from death. The death of Jesus on the cross is the beginning of christian life.

B. The Acts of the Apostles

Since Acts is the second volume of one work it should be understood for what it is: more correctly a sequel to Luke's gospel than a history of the early Church. Given this close relationship, we are not surprised to find that the composition of Gospel and Acts runs along parallel lines. The narrative of the ministry of Jesus is formed of two more or less equal parts: the first, covering the preaching in Galilee, centers in the Twelve and ends with the mission confided to the Twelve. The other part, the journey to Jerusalem, begins

Plan of Acts
INTRODUCTION (1:1-11)
A. I.   THE JERUSALEM CHURCH (1:12—5:42)
II.   THE FIRST MISSIONS (6—12)
III. BARNABAS AND PAUL (13:1—15:35)
B. IV. THE MISSION OF PAUL (15:36—19:20)
V.   THE PRISONER OF CHRIST (19:21—28:29)
EPILOGUE (28:30 f.)

with the mission charge to the Seventy, and has material not found in Matthew and Mark. Similarly, Acts has two parts: one in which Peter has a leading role and which looks to Jerusalem (1:1—15:35); the second, centered in Paul, breaks out of this geographical framework and turns towards Rome 15:36—28:31).

Progress of the Gospel

.In Acts, Luke is concerned with showing the triumphal progress of the Gospel throughout the whole known world. The plan of his work is dictated by the commission of the Risen Christ to his disciples: 'You shall be my witnesses in Jerusalem and in all Judea and Samaria and to the end of the earth' (Acts 1:8). He is especially interested in the passing of the preaching from the Jews to the Gentiles and in the progress of the Gentile mission. Behind the continuous spread of the Good News through the provinces of the Roman Empire he sees the power of the Holy Spirit.

Luke was aware that the Gentile mission had been set on foot before Paul began to play his part, and he knew that Paul was not the only architect of the Gentile Church. But, since his purpose was to portray the spread of the Church, he could not have chosen a more dramatic and effective way of doing so. For it is true that Paul the missionary and Paul the theologian has set his stamp on Christianity. And, as Christianity is grateful to Luke for his strikingly beautiful portrait of Jesus, it is also grateful for his portrait of Paul.

The Discourses.

The discourses play an important role in bringing out the significance of the events described in the narratives. Each stage in the historical development of the Church is marked by an accompanying discourse which indicates the corresponding development of christian thought.

At the very beginning, the risen Christ specifies the role of his apostles and maps out their activity; Peters' words in the upper room underline the importance of the Twelve. His discourse at Pentecost points to the meaning of the ecstatic phenomenon and the intervention of the Holy Spirit; it is also the first message addressed to the Jews by the group of apostles. This message is further developed in Peter's subsequent addresses (3:12-26; 4:8-12; 5:29-32; 10:34-43). His reception of Cornelius marks a turning point, for now the admission of Gentiles must be justified (11:5-17; 15:7-11). Stephen's speech provides a valuable insight into the frame of mind of the Hellenists. It also shows an incipient impatience with the demands of the Mosaic law and with the Temple ceremonies that eventually will lead to a rupture with Judaism and bring Christians to a full consciousness of their own separate identity. Philip (8:30-33) explicitly identifies the Suffering Servant of Is 53 with Christ.

Discourses effectively bring out the meaning of Paul's mission. After reading Acts 13:16-41 there is no doubt that the Apostle of the Gentiles anxiously longs for the conversion of the Jews of the Diaspora — he echoes the theme of Peter. His speeches at Lystra (14:15-17) and before the council of the Areopagus (17:22-51) show how he could accommodate himself to the style of hellenistic religious propaganda which owed much to Stoicism. His farewell address to the elders of Ephesus at Miletus (20:18-35) is the Apostle's testament. His later discourses, at Jerusalem (22:1-21; 23:1-6), at Caesarea (24: 10-21; 26:2-23), and at Rome (28:17-20, 25-28) are personal apologiae; yet, we may gather from them something of the situation of Christians in face of Judaism and of the Roman authorities.

The Holy Spirit

In his Acts of the Apostles Luke speedily introduces the Holy Spirit. During his earthly life Christ was the unique bearer of the Spirit. The promise of the Father now, quite explicitly, turns out to be the Spirit: the disciples will be baptized with the Holy Spirit. The parousia may be long delayed; there is, in the meantime, the dynamic presence of the Holy Spirit in the Church. And the Spirit initiates, empowers, and directs the spread of the Church. The powerful coming of the Spirit at Pentecost opens the last age, the era of the Church. The Holy Spirit is the gift of the final age and the fulfillment of the Risen One's promise. It marks the beginning of the world mission of the apostles. The Holy Spirit has been poured out on all flesh: the era of prophecy, of inspired preaching, has begun. The real proof of the presence and the power of the Spirit is the courageous preaching of the good news. The sending of the Holy Spirit at Pentecost is a foundation of the new christian community, but as with any foundation, it remains as the source of union and stability long after the initial ceremony of foundation-laying. The entire life of early Christianity is led and protected by the Spirit.

Luke, in one text at least (2:33) attributes the outpouring of the Spirit not to the Father but directly to the risen Lord. It follows that the presence of the Holy Spirit in the Church is the sign of Christ's present power and glory. But we are not dependent on a single text for christological reference. When we look to the wider context we discern that most of the Lucan statements about the Holy Spirit are christological; the Spirit is intimately related to Christ.

Jesus' promise that his disciples, when haled before their accusers would be aided by the Holy Spirit, was speedily verified in Peter's own case (4:8-12). And it was quickly verified that the experience of Pentecost was not a once-for-all event (4:31). The basis of apostolic witness is the presence of the Holy Spirit in the witness. Throughout Acts a requisite condition of one who might hold office is that he be 'full of the Spirit.' The fullness of the Spirit in Stephen explains at once his achievement, and the virulence of the opposition to him.

For Luke, the Spirit is sovereign and free, and active in the community of the Lord. The gift of the Spirit comes through the Church. This is a truth of major importance, but one which can be, and has been tragically exaggerated. Always, the whole New Testament witness has to be taken into account. If it is Luke's view that the Spirit is given through the accredited witnesses, John, just as authoritatively, reminds us that the Spirit 'blows where he wills.' We must never forget that God is greater than the Church and that divine condescension can never lead to a human harnessing of the Spirit.

The vitally important turn of the Gentile mission is emphatically the work of the Spirit. It could not be otherwise. The conversion of Cornelius involves a second Pentecost —a Gentile Pentecost. The Spirit came upon and designated Cornelius and his household; the rite of baptism incorporated them, visibly, into the christian community. The gift of the Spirit they had already received is a gift of the risen Lord.

The Lord had indicated that the mission must move from Jerusalem to the end of the earth: the missionaries Barnabas and Saul were directly designated by the Holy Spirit. They were to find that, step by step, their missionary progress would be guided and sustained. A vital stage was that of the 'Council' of Jerusalem. The issue was whether or not Christianity was to be a Jewish sect or a universal religion. The epochal decision was taken: 'It has seemed good to the Holy Spirit and to us.' The Gentile mission is, without doubt, the intent and the work of God.

The great apostle of the Gentiles found that he was not only a vessel of election, set aside by the Lord; he was to find that the course of his mission was explicitly delineated by the same Spirit. He was directed into Macedonia, pointed there by the Spirit of Jesus. The divine directives take different expression, but always it is the guidance of the Lord Jesus. The principal actor in Acts is neither Peter nor Paul, but the risen Lord, present as Spirit.

Yet again, in his 'Ephesian Pentecost,' Luke reminds us that the spread of the Church is the work of the Spirit. but the spreading Church must remain one; he stresses that the group of disciples of the Baptist, baptized and incorporated into the community by the accredited apostle Paul, straightway received the Holy Spirit and its manifest gifts. The Spirit, directly, and through christian prophets, intimated to Paul his path of affliction and imprisonment. For that matter, he saw himself as 'bound by the Spirit,' as he was, too, a prisoner of Christ Jesus. If the meat of the Lord was to do the will of him who sent him, so it was with Paul: his only concern was to do the will of the Master. He resolutely went to meet his fate. From first to last, his is the career of one guided by the Spirit.

Such is, in brief, Luke's teaching on the Spirit, the gift of God to us through the risen Christ. The early Christians were conscious that the Spirit of God was directing their lives in a special and consistent way. What about our own day with its rediscovery of the Holy Spirit? Has Luke got anything to offer us? 'All those who have discovered the power of the Spirit will find Luke's theology an incentive to further growth in their own life of the Spirit. It awakens us to the fact that the Holy Spirit is not merely a personal gift of God to each of us. It is a Spirit for mission to our fellowmen, a Spirit we learn to recognize and discern at work in the world, in the christian community, and in the gifts and insights of one another.' (J. McPolin).

C. The Pauline Letters.

The letters of St Paul are the earliest writings of the New Testament. On the whole, they are occasional writings, that is to say, written by the apostle in view of special circumstances affecting the particular church to which he wrote. In the traditional grouping of Pauline letters it is questionable whether Colossians and, even more doubtfully, Ephesians are his work. The Pastorals are even less likely to have come from him. And nobody, any longer, would maintain that Hebrews is by Paul.

1, 2 Thessalonians

Paul visited Thessalonica for the first time in the course of his second missionary journey, probably in the year 50 A.D. His stay was short — a matter of a few months. Later, in Corinth, being assured by his emissary Timothy that the young community was thriving, he gave expression to his relief in a letter to it (*1 Thessalonians*). He seized the occasion to draw attention to certain shortcomings and to issue instructions. This first (extant) letter sets the pattern for the subsequent Pauline letters. An address (1:1-2) is followed by a long thanksgiving (1:3-10) for the manifest fruits of a conversion wrought by the Spirit. He reminds the Thessalonians of his personal affection and concern (2:1-20). The second part of the writing, following the usual practice of Paul, takes up matters of personal import and exhorts the faithful to the practice of christian morality.

Paul's principal reason for writing another letter (*2 Thessalonians*) was to set right certain erroneous views on the Parousia. One practical issue was that some Thessalonians, expecting an imminent End, no longer saw any point in work. Paul dealt with these problems in forthright fashion. Both letters present christian life as a call by God to prepare for a share in the victory of Jesus by growing in faith, mutual love and the hope of the return of Jesus as Lord.

The Major Epistles

Four of Paul's writings — Galatians, 1 and 2 Corinthians, and Romans — (likely in that chronological order) are known as the Major Epistles. We shall take Galatians in close connection with Romans. Galatia had been evangelized by Paul early in his second missionary journey (50-52) and *Galatians* was most likely written during the apostle's stay in Ephesus (54-57). The purpose of the epistle is clearly defined: to refute the error of judaizers who had come to disturb the faith of the Galatians by teaching the necessity of the observance of the Mosaic Law; and, positively, to vindicate Paul's 'Gospel': justification through faith in Christ.

When Paul learned that the Galatian community was in danger of falling under the sway of judaizers and was looking to the false security of observance, he reacted violently . He insists on his authority, not to browbeat the Galatians, not to awe them into submission, but in an almost desperate effort to get them off their knees, to get them to accept the burden of responsibilty and take the risk of making decisions.

In Paul's view, the fundamental truth about Christianity is that it is a religion of *grace* and not of merit ('a different gospel,' 1:6). Troublemakers in Galatia were insisting that the way of standing right with God was by observance of rules. Paul saw this striving for merit as a distortion of the Good News. And there is no other version of the Good News apart from the gospel he had proclaimed.

Justification by faith.

In Gal 2:15-21 Paul gives a resumé of his gospel; much of the doctrine of Galatians and Romans is compressed into these few verses. The specific purpose of Galatians is to defend the doctrine of justification by faith in Christ without the works of the Law. The Jerusalem leaders he names were able to accept his stance because they too believed that salvation was from Christ alone. Nor did Paul object to the fact that the Judeo-Christians of Palestine remained faithful to the Mosaic observances. Yet he saw the inherent danger and realised that the full christian doctrine involved freedom from the Law in theory and in fact. We cannot win salvation by our own observances; we must accept it as free gift from Christ. The same basic teaching, in different terms — redemption by the death and resurrection of Christ — runs through the letter. Crucified with Christ, the Christian is dead to the Law in order to share in the life of the risen Christ (2:19); even while still in the flesh he is animated by the life of Christ and spirtualized through faith. 'I have been crucified with Christ' (2:20) Paul can assert because, through faith and baptism (Rom 6:3-11), the Christian has been identified with the phases of Jesus' passion, death and resurrection; he can therefore 'live to God.' He can declare 'Christ lives in me' because he experiences union with Christ, the glorified Lord, who has become at the resurrection 'a lifegiving Spirit' (1 Cor 15:45). This Christ is the vital principle of christian activity. Paul can further claim: 'I live by faith in the Son of God' because he realizes in faith that his real life comes from his surrender to the power of the Son of God within him. He is in love with that Son who loved him and died for him. He will not now insult that love by spurning the gracious gift of God and vainly strive to earn justification (v.21).

90

Christian freedom.

'For freedom Christ has set us free' (5:1). Paul, the former Pharisee, believed passionately in *freedom*. He had known, too long, the slavery of a rigid religious system, the bondage of a religion of law and precept. Christ had set him free from all that and he gloried in his freedom. He ached for his disciples to value the freedom that was theirs; he was sad, and angry, when freedom was not truly appreciated: 'stand fast, therefore, and do not submit again to the yoke of slavery' (v.1). He understood very well the awesome responsibility of freedom and scrupulously respected the conscience of his disciples. He would not compel them: they must make their own personal decisions. But christian freedom is never licence to do as one pleases; it is always motivated — and constrained — by love. 'For though I am free from all men, I had made myself a slave to all...' (1 Cor 9:19).

Romans

The issue raised in a polemical atmosphere in Galatians was taken up again by Paul in a letter which was meant to prepare his way for a visit to Rome (*Romans*, written at Corinth, winter 57/58). Paul is concerned to expound his Gospel, his manner of preaching the good news of Christ: his emphasis on the central truth of salvation. He shows that salvation, necessary for all and offered to all, is indeed presented to all by the preaching of the Gospel.

The Righteousness of God.

In Rom 3:21-31 Paul takes up the thesis which he has enunciated at the beginning of the Letter: 'For in it (i.e. the Gospel) the righteousness of God is revealed through faith for faith' (1:17). He now stresses that this has happened apart from the law since Christ, who is the essence of the Gospel, died as an outlaw. If one believes in Christ one could no longer maintain that right relationship (what the Jews called 'righteousness') with God was obtainable through the Law. In Paul's mind it is a question of either ... or. Before his conversion, zeal for the Law entailed the violent exclusion of Christ, afterwards, his attachment to Christ spelt the end of the law (except in so far as it was accomplished in Christ) as a means of 'justification.' He would maintain that the law itself and the prophets witness to this position.

Since all humankind (and Paul has spent some notable time illustrating this point, 1:8 — 3:20) have sinned, they are all — both Jew and Gentiles — sinners and, therefore, God's debtors. Nothing they can do is able to put them in right relationship with God. If, therefore, they are to be righteous at all, this can only be by sheer gift of God which is made in Christ. That is what Paul asserts in his uncompromising statement: 'we hold that a man is justified by faith apart from works of law.'

God's amazing love.

The passage 5:6-11 presents a favourite Pauline theme. God showed his love for men and women while they were still incapable of doing anything to help themselves. At the appropriate moment in the history of salvation he sent his Son who died on behalf of the sinful and the ungodly. This was the measure of God's love. To paraphrase v. 8: the proof of God's amazing love is that, while we were yet sinners and adrift from God, Christ the Son of God died for us, the ungodly.

Christ's death is a sign of God's love for humankind. The 'judgment' of God upon humankind, which looms largely in Romans, is about to break, but the one who is justified by faith need have no fear because, by definition, he is justified by God's grace. He already enjoys the 'favour' of his judge. The same love which justified him will also save him. The basically forensic character of righteousness here comes to the fore. The righteous man is one who is found or pronounced righteous by God in the judgment of the last days. But since no man is righteous in himself before God, he becomes righteous only because God declares him such. God's word is justifying and, since it always finds man in himself a sinner and unrighteous, necessarily salvific. God's righteousness is a saving righteousness. Hence the justified man knows that, as far as God is concerned, he is already saved in hope.

The love of Christ

Paul's triumphant hymn at the close of the third major section of the letter (8:31-39) makes the point with verve. From 5:6 to 8:30 his preoccupation has been to demonstrate to the believer God's love for humankind. He wants to show that redemption, what God has done for the world in Christ, is a work of God's love, that is, of his total self-giving in his Son. The application which Paul draws from that truth in this finale concerns the absolute assurance which the believer has of redemption. Paul has insisted sufficiently on the need for the believer's response to God's grace (6:1-23) to obviate an accusation of 'quietism.' But even this response is the work of God himself within the believer. As far as Paul is concerned 'all is grace.'

It is clear that Paul envisages himself and his fellow Christians as being in the 'dock' (vv 31-34). In the great trial before God who, he asks, is against me? After all, God is for us! He did not spare his own Son but gave him up for us all. Who then shall bring a charge? Who, indeed, since it is God who justifies (that is, pronounces a saving verdict)! Who shall condemn? Do we not have Christ — Christ who died, who was raised from the dead and is now our intercessor at God's right hand! Therefore, who shall separate us from the love of God? And Paul goes on to enumerate a double series of obstacles: the first (v.36) comprising the hardships of missionary life, the second (vv 38-39) being a list of cosmic powers drawn from myth and astrology. Nothing, he concludes, in all creation, will separate us from the love of God in Christ Jesus.

1 and 2 Corinthians

Paul, while at Ephesus (54-57), was informed of rival parties and of scandals in the Corinthian church; and the Corinthians, in a letter to him, had submitted a number of questions. Notable features of his reply (*1 Corinthians*) concern the christian attitude to marriage and celibacy, the authentic doctrine of the Eucharist, and the first appearance of his teaching on the Body of Christ. He uncompromisingly rejects the wisdom of the world, the foolish self-sufficiency of human thought. It is foolish because it ignores man's complete dependence on God; that is why he is desirous of knowing nothing except 'Jesus Christ and him crucified.'

Is Christ Divided?

It is clear from several references in the letter that the bond of brotherhood (and sisterhood) was under severe strain in Corinth. Apart from the jealousy and wrangling (3:3) that characterized the behaviour of the Corinthian Christians, there were rival factions among them. When he has completed his customary address and thanksgiving (1:1-9), Paul plunges into an appeal for unity in the community. To a community of such divided loyalties, Paul puts the rhetori-

cal question, 'Is Christ divided?' Furthermore, when com-
pared with Christ, who is Paul, or Apollos, or Cephas? They
are merely the servants of the Corinthian Christians (3:22-
23), Christ's servants entrusted with the mysteries of God
(4:1) who preach the Good News of Jesus crucified and
baptize into membership of his Body, the Church.

The folly of the cross.

While it may be that his experience of dismal failure at
Athens just before his departure for Corinth (Acts 17:32-33)
had influenced Paul's approach, it must be that the real
motivation of his uncompromising preaching of Christ
crucified was because he had come to a profound understanding of the Cross. He realized that here the ornate language of Greek oratory would be wholly out of place. The
gospel message, in its starkness, would speak for itself: God
redeemed the world through the death of his Son on a cross
and he, Paul, was sent by Christ to preach the Good News of
this redemption. By human standards it is foolishness: it is
folly to look for rdemption to one who could not save
himself from death. But the power of God that raised Jesus
from the dead is still at work in the world leading men and
women to faith in Christ. The cross, which must always be
central to Christianity, is the great sign of contradiction and
is the proof that Christianity survives and makes progress
through the power of God, not through the efforts of man.

The imitation of Christ.

A Christian gives glory to God by being what he or she is
meant to be: a manifestation of the love of Christ. Hence, one
must give no offense *to anyone.* One must never do anything
that would make it difficult for the Jew or the pagan to see
the beauty of Christianity. One's actions should never lead a

Christian to reject his church or be the reason of his failure to grow in holiness. Paul himself had always been guided by his consideration for the good of others and he urges the Corinthians to follow his example. The ultimate norm, for him and for them, is Christ 'who did not please himself' (Rom 15:3). In order to assure them that the ideal is not beyond the reach of humankind, Paul can say to the Corinthians: 'Be imitators of me, as I am of Christ' (11:1). The implication is awesome. To demonstrate to others that the love of God in Christ is a present reality a preacher should be able to point to himself. Paul, at least, would hold that if he cannot do so, if he cannot show forth in his person 'the life of Jesus' (2 Cor 4:10), he really has no right to speak.

2 Corinthians

In Macedonia, towards the close of 57, Paul learned that the turbulent Corinthian community, in the meantime shaken by further crises, was at last reasonably tranquil. *Second Corinthians* expresses his satisfction at this turn; but it is also very much of an apologia. The writing is, in large measure, a defence of the apostolic ministry and reveals the deeply human side of Paul. We find in him the model of a pastor: a fusion of love and of justice, of prudence and of energy in the animating and guiding of a community.

Paul seeks to re-establish the warm relationship that had existed between the Corinthian community and himself (cf 1 Cor 4:14-16). Rivals of his, 'traveling preachers,' more eloquent than he, less demanding in their moral standards, had attempted to come between him and the community. They accused Paul of promising a great deal by letter and doing little in person. He had been accused of vacillating, of saying one thing and of doing (or meaning) something else. Refuting the charge of duplicity, he declares himself not to

be a man who answer 'yes' and 'no' in the same breath. He is
very conscious that he is a sign of Christ, and Christ is
fidelity itself (1:15-22).

Afflicted but not crushed

In his first letter to the Corinthians (1:18-30) Paul had
spoken of the folly of the cross. The same idea runs through
2 Cor 4:6-11 — God works through human weakness so that
the success of the apostolate and the advance of the kingdom
of God will be seen as the work of God not of humankind.
The message is preached by weak 'servants of the word' like
himself to show that it is the power of God and not anything
in themselves that brings it to fruition. Their lives are
paradox, revealing the intimate nature of their ministry
which is to prolong in time the paschal mystery, the death
and resurrection of Jesus. They may be worn down by the
tribulations of the ministry but the life of Jesus flows from
them to others. What was true of the apostolate in Paul's
time remains true of the church in every generation. The all
too human character of christian ministers is no indication
that the church's mission will fail.

The driving force

Our appreciation of Paul will be increased when we understand that what is central to him is not so much a doctrinal
position as his experience of the boundless love of Christ.
This is the driving force behind his passionate, at times
polemical, interest in the christian communities for which
he feels himself responsible. The passage 5:11-21 brings us
close to the heart of Paul. The love of God stirs him and he,
in his turn, proclaims Christ, dead and risen again. Here he
gives the reason for Jesus' death not in cultic terms (as
sacrifice for sin) but in terms of human existence: Christ died

so that we should live a Christ-centred and no longer a self-centred life. Paul mentions one result of his new life in his own case; he no longer judges anyone by worldly standards and conventions. This goes, supremely, for his understanding of Christ (v.16). Before his conversion Paul would have looked upon Jesus as a man among men, 'according to the flesh.' On the Damascus road he encountered the risen Saviour.

The power of Christ.

Chapter 10-13 is Paul's letter written 'out of much affliction and anguish of heart and with many tears' (2:4) — a stirring and emotional defence of his apostolate and gospel. The Lord has called him to the apostolic ministry; this is approbation and praise enough; self-praise would sound foolish beside it (ch 10). Much of ch. 11 is bitingly sarcastic. Paul had been called a 'fool'; let them put up with his 'folly' then! He had been driven to self-defence by the fickleness of the Corinthians who were ready to accept a different gospel. Although boasting about visions is out of place, Paul is compelled to recall an extraordinary experience: he had found himself caught up to the divine presence (12:1-4). A keen reminder of his human weakness kept him from being carried away by the experience. He regarded his infirmity as an impediment to the effectiveness of his ministry and prayed to be rid of it. This was not to be and Paul realized that God's mysterious ways of salvation were at work in his own person.

What was important to him above all was the Lord's answer to his prayer: 'My grace is sufficient for you, for my power is made perfect in weakness.' The human limitations and disabilities of the sincere and generous apostolate are not an obstacle to apostolic work because the power of

Christ within 'is able to do far more abundantly than all we ask or think' (Eph 3:20). Indeed, insult, persecution, even calamity, may be vehicles of that power, a power all the more manifest because it works through the frailty of the apostle.

These are comforting words and challenging words for Christians and especially for those entrusted with the ongoing proclamation of Christ's message. To acknowledge our human weakness should not be an excuse for lapsing into a comfortable mediocrity. The love of Christ must be a driving force (cf 5:14) for his power is at it best in weakness. Paul's words proclaim to Christians that the enemy of the apostle is not humbling self-knowledge but thoughtless self-sufficiency.

We have lingered over the Major Epistles — as we did over the Gospels and Acts. We will have to make do with a brief glance at the other New Testament writings — not because they are not important but because one must keep this book within reasonable limits.

The Captivity Letters

The four letters, Philippians, Philemon, Colossians, and Ephesians are called the Captivity letters because they are, or purport to have been, written in prison. The church of Philippi was the one dearest to the heart of Paul and *Philippians* is remarkable for its spirit of joy and for its glimpse into the fatherly heart of the apostle. Of special interest and importance is the hymn (2:6-11) quoted by Paul — striking witness to the early emergence of a rich christology. In the little letter to *Philemon*, Paul, with notable delicacy, urges Philemon to welcome back as a brother his runaway slave Onesimus, now, too, a Christian. The onus is firmly on Philemon. A truly christian response must be free, not a matter of duress.

A dangerous error, seemingly sprung from a syncretistic Judaism, which would impair the role of Christ, had won some acceptance in the church of Colossae. The letter to the *Colossians* firmly asserts the absolute supremacy of Christ, beginning and end of creation, head of the Church which is his Body, mediator and universal redeemer. The related letter to the *Ephesians* develops these ideas. Now the Church, the Body of Christ, is seen reaching out to the limits of the new universe. This writing considers, too, the problem, raised in Romans, of the union of Jews and Gentiles. A serious question-mark stands over the Pauline authorship of Colossians and especially of Ephesians — both may well be pseudonymous. This means that a disciple of Paul, one who revered the great apostle, faced up to the problem and difficulties of his later age in the manner he believed Paul would have done in his own day. Of course, these letters, Pauline or not, are part of the New Testament and as fully Scripture as the rest.

The Pastorals

The two letters to *Timothy* and the letter to *Titus*, known as the Pastorals, are concerned with the organization and development of christian communities and with the qualities and responsibilities of those who minister to the christian people. Their author would seem not to have been an immediate disciple of Paul, but a man of the second, or it may be, third, christian generation. He has used the names of the well-known disciples to deal with the problems of the community, or communities, of his concern. Paul is, for him, the ideal apostle. And the pastoral directives, needful for his situation, found greater weight when they were presented as issuing from Paul.

100

Hebrews

The magnificent letter to the *Hebrews* was written by an unknown, immensely gifted, disciple of Paul, to encourage converts who, in face of difficulties and persecution, were tempted to drift from Christianity. The author exhorts them to cling to the Word of God as unveiled by Christ, and to preserve faith. The force of the argument rests altogether on the person and work of Jesus: Son of God, eternal high priest, offering a perfect sacrifice. (See pp. 127-133).

D. The Catholic Epistles

In addition to the collection of Pauline letters the New Testament contains another group of seven epistles: James, 1 and 2 Peter, 1, 2 and 3 John, and Jude. But these lettters differ so widely among themselves that the mere fact of not being 'Pauline' seems to be the only reason for grouping them. Their title Catholic Epistles is meant to imply the 'general' character of these writings: they are addressed to Christians in general (and not to invididual churches like the letters of Paul).

James is written to a milieu in which social differences are marked. The author's sympathy goes to the afflicted and weak. While he takes issue with injustice, poverty has for him a religious value which makes of the unfortunate the privileged friends of God. *1 Peter* was written to strengthen its recipients in their faith. Christians, in their trials, will be comforted and supported by the example of Jesus, by his meekness in the face of suffering unjustly inflicted. The author of *Jude* takes issue with false teaching and unmasks some who would pervert the traditional doctrine and put the faith of the community in peril. The writer of *2 Peter* is concerned that his readers should not lose their promised entry into the eternal kingdom of Jesus Christ and he writes

101

to strengthen them in the traditional faith — taking to task teachers who might lead them astray. The three *Epistles of John* show a striking resemblance among themselves and with the Fourth Gospel; the first of the three is far and away the most important. *1 John* is addressed to those 'who believe in the name of the Son of God': the author's primary purpose is to make his readers understand the sublimity of their condition as Christians. A writing of elevated spirituality, it keeps a close and constant grip on the world of men and testifies to a simple but demanding moral realism: fellowship with God, participation in the divine life, is impossible without generous fidelity to the Commandment.

E. The Book of Revelation

Like the book of Daniel, the *Revelation* of John was written in a troubled time and for a special purpose, and like Daniel, it carries a message that reaches beyond the immediate crisis. Revelation is at once a declaration of christian faith and hope and a full-blooded attack on the official paganism of Rome. The author is a witness, and he speaks with the authority of the former prophets sent by God — and he echoes their words and images. His book is a commentary on the reassuring words of Jesus to his disciples: 'In the world you have tribulation; but be of good cheer, I have overcome the world' (John 16:33). (See pp. 133-142).

From first to last, the New Testament, in the sublimity and in the relevance of its message, bears witness to the activity of the Spirit whom the risen Lord had sent, the Spirit who had inspired the first christian preachers and the chosen writers.

Chapter Five

The Newness of the New Testament

In his epistle to the Romans St. Paul develops his understanding of salvation and of the christian life. He teaches that the Gospel, understood as integral Christianity, is the sole efficacious saving force: 'It is the power of God for everyone who has faith, to the Jew first, and also to the Greek' (Rom 1:16). The whole of the New Testament, and not Paul only, proclaims this message of salvation. The Old Testament is, to be sure, the Word of God; it is, indeed, God's revelation: 'In many and various ways God spoke of old to our fathers by the prophets' (Heb 1:1). But now there is a new dimension to God's self-revelation: 'but in these last days he has spoken to us by a Son' (1:2). In the fullness of time the Son of God came forth, born of a woman (Gal 4:4). The creative and revealing Word which issued from the mouth of God, the Wisdom of God which the sages of Israel had celebrated, now had, most wonderfully, appeared on earth: 'the Word became flesh and dwelt among us' (Jn 1:14). Full of grace and truth, he grants the divine sonship to those who believe in him (1:10-14). The expectation of the Old Testament is fulfilled: the Messiah has come, God's final age has dawned.

The Kingdom

In a summary statement, early in his gospel, Mark gives the burden of the initial preaching of Jesus in Galilee: 'The time is fulfilled and the kingdom of God is at hand; repent and believe in the glad tidings' (Mk 1:15). In speaking of the kingdom of God Jesus spoke of something already familiar to his hearers: God's expected definitive incursion into our history. What is wholly new is that in Jesus, in his words and works, this presence of God is a reality here and now.

Especially in his parables Jesus presented the kingdom — God's reign — showing its presence and its growth, painting the dispositions of those who would enter into it, warning those who opposed it of their plight and, at all times, urging the mercy and love of the kingdom's King. The central fact remains that the kingdom had come. But it had come quietly, unnoticed. It is like a seed that must germinate, a plant that must spring up and grow. This seed, sown by God, will ripen to an abundant harvest. Like leaven in a mass of dough it will permeate the world of men. Jesus is the kingdom — and those who belong to him enter it with him and through him.

The Father

The Bible opens with the God who made all things, a transcendent God who is nevertheless deeply involved in the world he has shaped. Jesus has brought this God immeasurably nearer to us. In the New Testament God emerges as a vulnerable God, a loving Father. He is a prodigal Father to an estranged world of men: 'God so loved the world that he gave his only Son' (Jn 3:16). He himself is fully involved in the giving, the handing over, of his Son. Our Father is the Father of our Lord Jesus Christ. His glory is seen on the face of Jesus, his vulnerability in the cross of Jesus.

Luke tells us that Jesus, who had witnessed the power of God at work through his disciples (10:17-20) rejoiced in the Holy Spirit and then declared, 'All things have been delivered to me by my Father; and no one knows who the Son is except the Father, or who the Father is except the Son and any one to whom the Son chooses to reveal him' (Lk 10:21-22; Mt 11:25-27). This saying, so reminiscent of John, clearly expresses the unique relationship of Father and Son. The prologues of two other New Testament writings tell us why the Son alone can reveal the Father. John declares: 'No one has ever seen God; God only-begotten who is in the bosom of the Father, he has made him known' (Jn 1:18). And the author of Hebrews informs us that God, who had spoken variously through the prophets, has uttered his final word by a Son who 'reflects the glory of God and bears the very stamp of his nature' (Heb 1:3). The inevitable conclusion, of immense practicality for the christian life, is that we cannot find God except in and through Jesus. The Son alone can make the Father known, can lead us to him. This he has expressly declared: 'I am the way, and the truth, and the life; no one comes to the Father but by me' (Jn 14:6).

The Son

Who is this Son of God who reveals to us the Father? The whole of the New Testament is concerned to make him known. In the light of the Resurrection the disciples began to grasp who and what Jesus of Nazareth really was — Christology was born. Theirs was a formidable task: to reconcile their growing conviction of the divine status of the risen Lord with their uncompromising monotheism. But their Spirit-born conviction of who Jesus was drove them to formulate their faith. So, starting with the Resurrection, they pushed back the moment of divine Sonship to the Baptism (Mark), to the conception of Jesus (Luke and Matthew) and eventually to pre-existence (John) — for incarnation is the answer. The man Jesus of Nazareth is truly Son of God because he is none other than the Word made flesh. He is God's response to the Fall. God, in him, has come to show us what authentic humanness is. Our response must surely be to strive to be truly human. 'Learn of me . . .'.

The Spirit

Throughout the Old Testament the Spirit is the presence and the power of Yahweh — his dynamic presence. In the New Testament the Spirit is, largely, the power and presence of the risen Lord. We, naturally enough, think of Holy Spirit in the context of a developed trinitarian theology. The idea of a Trinity of Persons appears nowhere in the Old Testament. Nor even in the New Testament is a trinitarian doctrine of one God in three persons at all obvious. We are prone to read back into Scripture the categories of a later theology. In point of fact, in the New Testament, 'Holy Spirit' does not clearly emerge as a person; not, at least, as a person sharply distinct from the Lord. We have indicated, briefly, a growth in christological thinking. It needed time, too, for the early Christians to evaluate the implication of the undoubted presence of the Holy Spirit within and among them. For if, in the pages of the New Testament, the concept of the Holy Spirit will prove elusive, we shall not fail to recognize an unmistakeable fact: the conviction of a pervasive presence of the Holy Spirit.

If the New Testament fails to provide us with a neat trinitarian doctrine, it does something much more. It puts before us a concerned and caring Father: 'God so loved the world that he gave his only Son' (Jn 3:16). It gives us a Son of flesh and blood: 'The Word became flesh and dwelt among us' (1:14). It shows us a Spirit pervasive and active, making Father and Son to dwell within us. It is the richness and warmth of our God.

The Church

Jesus sought to gather together a community of salvation: in a wealth of pictures he spoke of this new people of God. His favorite is that of the description of the community as the family of God, a family that finds its communion in eucharistic table-fellowship in anticipation of the heavenly feast. This new people was animated and encouraged by a keen awareness of the boundlessness of God's grace. We can grasp what the Resurrection really meant to these men: now they were truly new — new men in a new world, confident, courageous, and enterprising. For they had this tremendous sense of being 're-created'.

The contemporary Church, and the Church of the future, can only remain true to its own nature if it understands itself to be the Church of the apostolic age; for it is only through the apostolic Church and its testimony to the faith that the Church reaches back to Jesus Christ. The 'apostolic age', the first age of the Church, does not only mark a beginning in time: it is the foundation of the Church. The Church must grow, it must develop over the centuries; but the edifice of the Church must always stand solidly on that foundation. To change the metaphor, there is a norm, and authentic growth can be measured against that norm.

107

The New Testament, incomplete and not clearly-defined though it be, is normative for the Church. And the Spirit, now as then, is present and active in the Church — in a human Church. But not everything is necessarily touched by the Spirit. What is wholly human is transient and will not last. Only what has been touched by the Spirit will remain.

Christian Life

We need not only to remind ourselves, but to learn as a living reality, that Christianity is, exists, because of Christ, and for no other reason at all. We need to take, with utmost seriousness, the realism of Paul and John. For them christian life is a new creation, a new birth. I am a Christian because Christ lives in me, because his life quickens me; I am a Christian because I am a branch of him, the true Vine, livened by the living sap of him. I am not a Christian *primarily* because I have been initiated into this society of his disciples, because I worship around the table of the Lord, because I seek to love my neighbor as he has commanded. I am a Christian in and through fellowship with him. Everything else follows on that. But it must necessarily follow on it. Through him I have fellowship with the Father. He is the bond who binds Christians together into the one Body. Christian life, because it is Christ-life, must be incarnational. It is lived in and through community.

The Message

This is surely the message of the New Testament. The gospels, all of them, are written that we may believe, and go on believing, that the man Jesus of Nazareth is the Messiah of Jewish hope — more, that he is the Son of God. They are

108

written that, through faith, we may have life in him. Paul's gospel is the good news of salvation by faith alone: openness to the salvation offered by God in Jesus Christ, and commitment to him. And Paul came to realize that though it must seem folly and scandal, the christian message is always Christ, a crucified Christ. The author of Hebrews can find no more effective way of calling back his readers from the brink of apostasy than by holding up before them Christ, the living high priest. The Revelation of John was written to encourage Christians faced with persecution. It was meant to assure them that Jesus had indeed overcome the world. It insists that christian victories can be won in one way only, the way in which he won his victory: through suffering and death. The Pastorals, with their concern for orthodox doctrine and their interest in incipient ecclesiastical office, reach beyond the apostolic age. They are still quite sure that there is one Mediator only between God and men: the man Christ Jesus (1 Tim 2:5). The first letter of John puts the New Testament view, the christian view, with simple and chilling clarity: 'God gave us eternal life, and this life is in his Son. He who has the Son has life; he who has not the Son has not life' (1 Jn 5:11-12).

Chapter Six

The Flavor of the New Testament

A survey of the books of the New Testament gives some indication of what it is about. But a closer look at particular areas will suggest more fully its variety and depth, will give the feeling and the taste of it.

A. Parables

The Setting

Jesus taught in parables. The gospel parables generally show traces of a two-fold, and often of a three-fold setting: the ministry of Jesus, the setting in the life of the early Church, an evangelist's editorial setting. The first setting entails what Jesus had said in what circumstances and how his original hearers had understood him. The second concerns what words the first Christians heard, and what they understood by them, when the parables had been handed down to them by oral tradition. The third setting comes into question when an evangelist, in keeping with his own theological outlook, fits a parable into his editorial plan.

The gospels bear abundant witness to the fact that the first Christians turned to the parables of Jesus as to living words which spoke directly to themselves. Already we are assured that we, too, should hear them as spoken to us. But we must begin by understanding. We must discern, if we can, the original import of a parable; we must look for any sign of adaptation or re-interpretation in the early preaching tradition; we must appreciate the purpose of an evangelist in his choice and presentation of any particular parable. For, if we are to be guided by, and live by, the words of Jesus, we must be sure that our application of his words to ourselves and to our situation is along the right lines. The evangelists are our guides.

Parables of Jesus

Jesus taught in parables. But what precisely is a 'parable'? A parable is a narrative having two levels of meaning and its purpose is to instruct — or, more properly — to challenge decision and invite action. The parable of The Prodigal Son, for instance, is not a story featuring an indulgent father; it is meant to illustrate God's boundless mercy towards the sinner. More than that — for there are two sons — it was meant by Jesus as a challenge to the Pharisees (represented by the elder son). (See p. 45) Because of this essential double-meaning aspect, the parable has (or may have) something mysterious above it: the hearer may be unable, or unwilling, to grasp the vital secondary level of meaning. This is why the parables are unsuitable for children below a certain mental age: they cannot yet make the transition from the story to its indirect meaning — and so they miss the point.

A parable may be an explanatory story, for instance, The Good Samaritan, Dives and Lazarus, The Pharisee and The Tax Collector(Lk 10:29-37; 16:19-31; 18:9-14).Or, it may be an allegorical story, for instance, The Prodigal Son (Lk 15:11-32), and The Unmerciful Servant (Mt 18:21-25). This point is important. It had been customary to make a

111

sharp distinction between parable and allegory and to write off as inauthentic (not going back to Jesus) anything that smacked of allegory. But there was confusion here. Allegory (where the details of a story have symbolic value as in The Wicked Vinedressers, Mk 12:1-8) is extended metaphor and, as such, is a story that has both a literal and a metaphorical level. An allegorical story can well be a parable — and it may not. A parable, whether it be allegory or exemplary story, has a specific religious or ethical purpose. An allegory need have no such purpose. There is no reason why an authentic parable of Jesus may not be an allegory. Other criteria must be sought for discerning whether or not any parable is, or is not, a parable of Jesus. The fact that a given parable is an allegorical story cannot, by itself, settle the matter. Jesus' intent was to challenge attitudes and invite commitment. He was not to be hampered by academic niceties.

Living words

Yet, from the first, his parables have been 're-translated'. It is this process which has shaped them into their present form in our gospels. To understand the parables through the continuous re-translation given them in their transmission down the centuries is to grasp how they continue to be Jesus' living word, addressed to every community of every present moment. For, the whole force of the parables lies in their showing the listener himself, confronting him with his own world. It becomes clear that the way in which Christians, from the beginning, have understood and responded to the parables, does provide a valid way of discerning their authentic message. Perhaps this is because no matter how much the early kerygmatic preaching or later christian preachers have adapted or even accommodated the parables, no one and nothing could deepen their essential message. For at their heart stands Jesus himself.

Parables in Mark

In chapter 4 of Mark (more precisely Mk 4:1-34) we find a collection of parables and, in vv. 10-12 the evangelist's theory of the purpose of parables. It would seem that he presents a rigidly determinist view: there are those who, divinely enlightened, understand and accept the message of the parables, while 'those outside' fatally misunderstand and reject. Mark has capitalized on the mysterious aspect of the parables: they are necessarily 'mysterious' for those who will not listen. He is facing up to a problem which so exercised the early Church: the obduracy of Israel (cf Rom 9-11). But he has in mind all who rejected the teaching of Jesus and the preaching of the apostles. His point is that, to understand and accept the person and teaching of Jesus, one must be enlightened by the Holy Spirit. For those whose 'hardness of heart', whose resistance to the good news, puts up a barrier to the invitation and challenge of Jesus, the parables are riddles. They do not understand, because they will not.

Suffering

The issue, for Mark, is 'the secret of the kingdom of God'. This secret, as his whole gospel conveys, is the mystery of victory through suffering: 'the Son of man must suffer many things' (8:31). The privileged disciples (and the readers of Mark) know the secret, but the other are in the dark. 'Everything happens in parables' explains to the disciples — and the readers — why Jesus speaks of himself and of the kingdom in parables, and only in parables (v. 34). It requires enlightenment, presupposing goodwill and openness, to understand that suffering can, and normally must be, part of christian living. Mark's theory of parables is of a piece with his total gospel presentation. 'If any man would come after me, let him deny himself and take up his cross and follow me' (Mk 8:34).

Parables in Matthew

The pivotal position of chapter 13 in Matthew's gospel, and its emphasis on parables and their interpretation, make the chapter a crucial test of the redaction-critical method of gospel study — the analysis of an evangelist's specific contribution. What we find in this chapter is that as Jesus used parables to meet the demands of his own situation, so does Matthew use them to meet the needs of the community, the church, to which he belonged. He has put the parables of chapter 13 at the service of his own age and of his own theology.

The context

We need to glance at the context of chapter 13. It turns out that this parable section forms the second part of the coherent whole 11:2 - 13:52. The first part (chs 11-12) records the mounting opposition to Jesus, and his rejection. This is underlined by the words of thanksgiving for the revelation to 'babes' of what remains hidden to the 'wise and understanding' (11:23-24), and culminates in the passage about the 'true relatives' of Jesus, those who do the will of the Father (12:46-50). Then, in 13:1-35, Jesus addresses 'the crowds' as representing the whole of unbelieving Judaism (chs 11-12); those who are blind, deaf, lacking understanding (13:10-13). Thus, Matthew is saying that the first half of Jesus' parable discourse is an apologia; it is his reaction to

114

his having been rejected by the Jews. But the second half of the discourse (13:36-52) marks a sudden shift to the *disciples* (13:36). They are such as do God's will (12:49-50). Jesus instructs them as to what doing God's will really means.

The Lord speaks

Matthew construes 13:36-52 as an address of Jesus Kyrios, the risen and living Lord, to his Church, and his intention is exhortatory. In the interpretation of the parable of the weeds (13:37-43) the Lord exhorts the Christians of Matthew's community to be sons of the kingdom who do God's will. Doing the will of God is not easy. Christians have 'found' the kingdom: they must stand by their find, at the price of total commitment (the parables of The Treasure and The Pearl). Their situation is one marked by urgency — not even the Church will be saved from the great Judgment. Therefore Christians must continue to do God's will if they are to escape the fate of the godless (parable of The Net, 13:47-50). The question is, do the members of the community understand this (v. 51). 'Understanding' involves knowing the will of God and doing it with single-hearted devotion. As a householder brings out of his storeroom things new and old, so the disciple, in that he knows and does God's will, draws from his heart the revelation God has imparted to him through Jesus, the Lord.

Matthew's procedure in his chapter 13 is a prime example of the practical adaptation of parables. He is not at all concerned to present a Jesus of the past preaching to the crowds and teaching the disciples in Galilee. The evangelist is writing for his community, most of whom had never known Jesus 'in the flesh' (cf 2 Cor 5:16). But for him, as for them, the Lord is still present. His words still ring out, with immediate relevance, to those later hearers of his message. The characters, all of them, are contemporary: the living Lord, the Church, the Israel that has missed its way. These parables are not an echo from the past. They are the vibrant words of one who lives (cf Rev 1:8).

Parables in Luke

In Luke's mind the two parables of his chapter 16 (The Astute Steward and Dives and Lazarus) have the same theme: the use of money. The Astute Steward (16:1-8) is to teach the disciples (v. 1) the proper use of money; Dives and Lazarus (16:19-31) is to point out to the Pharisees the danger in which they stand by selfishly hoarding their wealth (v. 14). We are meant to see in Dives an example of a slave of Mammon. He is not a miser. If he is attached to his wealth it is because of the sumptuous life-style it enables him to maintain. But he is attached to it, with an attachment which leaves no place for God. We should not disassociate the parable of The Astute Steward from the companion parable of Dives and Lazarus in the same chapter. Instead, we might say that 16:9 teaches that Dives could and should have made a friend of Lazarus, a friend who could then introduce him to the eternal dwellings.

The rich

But we must look to the broader context of Luke's attitude towards wealth. Why is it 'easier for a camel to enter the eye of a needle than for a rich man to enter the kingdom of God' (18:25)? The first 'Woe' replies: because the rich 'have received their consolation' (6:24). The declaration of Abraham is more explicit: 'Son, remember that you in your lifetime received your good things, and Lazarus in like manner evil things; but now he is comforted here, and you are in anguish' (16:25). There is no doubt that Luke regarded the rich as unhappy and he invites us to pity them. The broad way along which they walk is not the path which leads to the Kingdom. Yet, the further question must be asked: is the misfortune of the rich attached to the wealth which they possess, or to that attitude of mind which wealth creates in them?

Security

In chapter 12 Luke leads us to the heart of the matter. There the parable of The Rich Fool, which warns against the tendency of seeking security in earthly wealth (12:15-21), must not be taken in isolation from the following development (vv. 22-34). Here, addressing his *disciples,* Jesus puts them on their guard, not against the danger of wealth which obviously does not threaten them (because they are poor), but simply against the normal anxiety of the poor, that for the food and clothing needful for life. In dreaming of his full barns, the rich man had a feeling of *security* (v. 19). On the other hand, the disciples who possess nothing, vividly feel their insecurity (vv. 22,29). There is no question of condemning this need for security inherent in the human situation. Rather, the intention is to show that the need goes astray when it seeks its support in earthly things. There is no authentic security that is not founded on God, on a vivid consciousness of his fatherly solicitude. There is no suggestion that wealth is an evil in itself, independently of the disposition of heart which it engenders in the rich. Wealth is a misfortune because it not only makes one indifferent to the good of the future life and prevents the rich from taking due account of their obligations in regard to the poor; but also because it tends to develop in the rich

117

a feeling of security which is radically incompatible with the trust which God claims for himself alone.

Warning

The parable of The Astute Steward (16:1-8) was one which Jesus' hearers would have readily understood. They would have appreciated the humor of his bold characterization: his putting forward of a disreputable man as a spur to resolute decision and action. Outside of Palestine the parable quickly raised the problem of how this unscrupulous man could be, in any sense, an example. The verses 10-13 are meant to answer the difficulty raised by the steward's conduct. He is no longer an example but a warning. It is noteworthy that these additions leave the substance of the parable unchanged, but they do bear witness to the interpretation of a parable which is now applied by the early Church to the community. It is, however, an application that is very much in the line of the parable as Jesus spoke it. The resolute action which he recommends does embrace the generosity of v. 9, the faithfulness of vv. 10-11, and the rejection of mammon in v. 13. The early Christians did not miss the point of the parable but, applying it to themselves, they necessarily caused a shift of emphasis. They were able to bring its teaching to bear on their daily lives because they lived in the atmosphere of the decision it urgently enjoined: they had accepted the Kingdom.

The use of money

Luke is more precise. In 16:1-9 the astute steward, a dishonest man (v. 8), is brought forward to teach Christians the wise use of money: to make friends with it, so that at death, when money fails, their friends can welcome them (their benefactors) into eternal dwellings. To use money wisely is to give it to the poor and so ensure one's eternal lot. The woe of the rich is linked to the horizon on which their eyes are fixed: 'Where your treasure is, there will your heart be also' (12:34). And even if the rich hear the word 'the cares and riches and pleasures of life choke them, and their fruit does not mature' (8:14). Their 'hearts are weighed down with dissipation and drunkenness, and cares of this life' (21:34). They become incapable of looking beyond this present life. Such is the conviction of Luke.

The parable of The Astute Steward says in positive terms what the parable of The Rich Fool says negatively. The steward is, at least, prudent: his example teaches people to use their earthly goods for the sake of a heavenly future. Just as the 'Woes' are addressed to the rich, the case of The Rich Ruler illustrates the extreme difficulty a rich man faces in finding salvation (18:18-27). The case of Zacchaeus shows that an exception is always possible. Jesus declares to him in effect: 'Today salvation has come to this house' (19:9). But in Luke's narrative this verdict is strictly linked to the declaration of the rich tax-collector, 'Behold, Lord, the half of my goods I give to the poor; and if I have defrauded anyone of anything, I restore it fourfold' (v. 8). Zacchaeus is saved but his fortune is gone back to the poor, and to those who have been the victims of his exactions. Inexorably, Luke maintains his position that the proper use of wealth is to distribute it to the poor.

God or Mammon

Even though the sayings of 16:9-13 are complementary to the parable of The Astute Steward, it is not unfair to say that the ultimate message of the parable, as Luke understands it, is given in v. 13 — 'No servant can serve two masters; for either he will hate the one and love the other, or he will be devoted to the one and despise the other. You cannot serve God and Mammon'. It is not simply a question of two ways of using money, but of the impossibility of any compromise between the service of God and the service of wealth — for Mammon takes on the character of an idol. Yet, it is not really a struggle between God and Mammon. The conflict is situated in the heart of man, in the psychological inability of giving himself wholly to two masters, neither of whom can be served by half-measures. The service of the one or of the other must be exclusive. One has to make a choice. The situation of the wealthy man is tragic: his wealth ties him to Mammon. How difficult it is to free himself and put himself wholly at the service of God. And thus Luke's closing recommendation remains: 'I tell you, make friends for yourselves of unrighteous mammon . . .'.

B. Beatitudes

Our gospels have two, notably different, versions of the beatitudes: Matthew 5:3-12 and Luke 6:20-23. Matthew has nine beatitudes. Luke has only four — but with four corresponding 'woes' (6:24-26). Both versions have grown from an original core going back to Jesus, the additions and adaptations being due to the evangelists.

The Beatitudes of Jesus

We can, without much trouble, discern a form of the beatitudes which would stand as a common basis for the developments of the evangelists and which may reasonably be regarded as representing the beatitudes of Jesus. These are three:

> Blessed are the poor, for the kingdom of heaven is
> theirs.

120

Blessed are those who hunger, for they will be filled.
Blessed are the afflicted, for they will be comforted.

The beatitudes do not refer to three different categories but
to three aspects of the same distressful situation. The first
sets the tone, and it echoes Is 61:1-2 (cf Lk 4:16-20). In de-
claring the poor blessed, Jesus gives concrete expression to
the Good News which he brings to the poor. The other two
beatitudes make more precise, and develop, the content of
the first. Our English word 'poor' is not the same as 'indigent'. In the gospels, the poor are the indigent, those who
depend totally on alms — they are the hungry. There is a
further nuance, that of the *anawim*, the lowly, the humiliated, those who are incapable of helping themselves and
are dependent on others. For these unfortunate ones the
proclamation of the coming of the Reign of God is truly
good news. The radical changes involved in the coming of
the Kingdom augur the end of their sufferings: those who
hunger will have plenty; those who are afflicted will be
consoled.

The poor

But what does it mean to be the privileged ones of the Kingdom? Many Christians are disturbed by the question. Why is
it that the poor should be better than others? What *merit* is
there in being poor, in being hungry? The question is, of
course, wide of the mark. It is not a matter of the merits of
the distressed but, rather, of the manner in which God
exercises his kingship. In Israel there was total agreement
on this point: the reign of God will achieve what one would
expect of the ideal reign. A good king will ensure the welfare of his subjects. And this means, in practice, that the good
king will be the champion of the weak and the poor, of the

defenseless. The 'blessedness' of the poor is in their very need, in their distress.

In the context of Jesus' preaching, the beatitudes were addressed to the poor and the unfortunate, quite generally, and in respect of their suffering situation. The beatitudes are an expression of the Good News: the Reign of God is near — God is about to exercise his royal power. They show us a God who will not remain neutral in the face of concrete human situations. In view of his royal prerogative, God takes the side of the weak against the strong, the side of the poor against the rich, the side of the oppressed against the oppressor,

The Beatitudes in Luke — and the Woes

Luke and Matthew have in common the three beatitudes of Jesus. They have also in common a fourth: the blessedness of those who suffer persecution for the sake of Christ. This was likely added in the tradition but, for practical purposes, we may regard it as a beatitude of Luke. In relation to the other three common beatitudes this one is at once similar and dissimilar. It is similar in that it speaks of people who suffer and whose situation offends God's justice. It is different in that it is no longer addressed to unfortunate ones in general but to those who suffer 'on my account' (Matthew), 'on account of the Son of man' (Luke). These are Christians who are blessed precisely because they suffer on account of their attachment to Christ.

Afflicted Christians

In Luke's version of the beatitudes this standpoint of the beatitude of the persecuted because of Christ is extended to the previous beatitudes which now also directly call to christian readers. Jesus had spoken to the poor as such, the afflicted and the hungry; their very distress was enough to make them privileged before God. Luke has applied these promises to his christian readers, with the manifest desire of encouraging them in their own painful situation. The beatitudes are now addressed to poor Christians. The promised blessedness will wonderfully compensate them for their present privations. But they ultimately owe their blessedness to their status as disciples of Christ.

In Luke's vocabulary the 'poor' are the indigent, people who lack the necessities of life. The 'hungry' are the poor considered in the concrete circumstances of their lives; they have not the wherewithal to obtain food. In contrast the 'rich' are those whose possessions isolate them from need; they are sheltered from hunger, the lot of the poor. The 'full' are people who are fully satisfied. These terms illustrate the realism of Luke's assessment of the respective situations of rich and poor. Deprived of material goods, and by themselves unable to obtain these goods, the poor are faced with lack of food — while the rich enjoy a prosperity that enables them to gratify their desires.

The 'laughter' of the third woe expresses the satisfied wellbeing of the fortunate ones of the world; the 'tears' of the third beatitude express the distress of those who know in their world only privation and suffering. The beatitude is addressed to unhappy people, crushed by their circumstances. Again, in the fourth woe the 'flattered' are the fortunate ones while the 'reviled' are suffering and persecuted Christians.

Encouragement
Luke fixed his attention on the implication of the beatitudes: they clarify the mission of Jesus, the role of Savior

which he is called upon to exercise in favor of those who believe in him, especially in favor of those who suffer for their faith in him. These beatitudes now apply to Christians in the painful conditions which persecution brings. This narrowing is a practical pastoral manner of coping with a crisis-situation. In Luke's catechesis the beatitudes become a means of encouraging believers in the midst of the difficulties in which they are caught. In their distress, the victims of persecution assuredly have the right to apply to themselves the consoling promises of the beatitudes.

The Beatitudes in Matthew

Matthew's longer version contains only three really new beatitudes: the merciful, the pure in heart, the peacemakers. We get a total of nine only because those of the poor/meek and the last two (the persecuted) are duplicates.

Poor in spirit

The expression 'poor in spirit' points to a transformation of the idea of 'the poor'. In current usage, the designation 'poor in spirit' would apply to one who is detached from worldly goods, who is interiorly free in regard to money. In fact, it is frequently related to the *possession* of wealth: it is possible for an economically rich man to be 'poor in spirit'. This is because *we* take 'poor' in a specific sense, an economic sense — which need not be the biblical meaning. And that meaning, we now know from the Jewish texts of Qumran, is 'humility'; the poor in spirit are the humble. The parallel beatitude of 'the meek' confirms this meaning. These beatitudes are, in Matthew, no longer addressed to those who lack the necessities of life, but to those characterized by their meekness, their patience, their humility.

This transposition harmonizes with an aspect of Matthew's portrait of Jesus; for only in Matthew do we find a saying of Jesus which is very close to the double beatitude:

Come to me, all who labor and are heavy-laden, and I will give you rest. Take my yoke upon you, and learn from me, for *I am meek and lowly in heart*, and you will find rest for your souls (11:28-29).

Thus the formulation of the first beatitude reflects the person of Jesus, his own attitude and sentiment. The demand to show oneself poor in spirit, and meek, is to model oneself on a Master meek and lowly in heart. It is evident that 'blessed are those who hunger and thirst for righteousness' is very different from Luke's blessedness of 'poor' and 'hungry'. For Matthew, Christianity has broadened and deepened the meaning of the term 'righteousness': 'Unless your righteousness exceeds that of the scribes and Pharisees you will never enter the kingdom of heaven' (5:20).

Intent and deed

Among the really new beatitudes we first look at 'Blessed are the pure in heart for they shall see God' (5:8). The qualification 'in heart' — like 'in spirit' — points to an interior disposition. What is in question is interior purity. It is what we would call 'purity of intention', demanding perfect correspondence between intention and action. The beatitudes of the merciful and of the peacemakers are concerned with action: the conduct of a Christian towards a neighbor who stands in need. The best illustration of 'merciful' is Matthew's description of the last judgment: 'I was hungry and you gave me food . . .' (25:35-40). As for the reference to 'peacemakers', it evokes a good work highly esteemed in

125

Judaism. It was observed that, among those who need help, the most needy are often an estranged husband and wife, or friends who have quarreled. To seek to reconcile them, to restore them to peace, is one of the kindest services one can render to the neighbor.

Where Luke applied the beatitudes to the Christians as a suffering minority, Matthew has introduced a distinction: he reserves the blessedness promised by the beatitudes to Christians who truly live the gospel ideal. He had re-read the beatitudes in the light of his pastoral preoccupations — and he had filled them out. He takes care to remind Christians that the promises of salvation are conditional (5:20). We will not be admitted to the Kingdom unless, after the example of the Master, we have shown ourselves to be meek and humble; unless we have given proof of righteousness and loyalty; unless we have carried out what God has asked of us — in particular, unless we have served our brethren in their need.

The line of continuity

At each stage, the beatitudes are a proclamation of blessedness. While pointed to the future of the Kingdom of God, they speak of a present blessedness. There is no question of seeking to escape the present or of taking refuge in a utopia; it is rather a question of being sensitive to the relationship between the present moment and God's future. The painful constraints which presently weigh on men, the demands to which Christians must here and now respond, constitute the soil in which grows the joyful hope that can transform the life of the believer. The beatitudes ring with a message of hope not in spite of the realities of life but in the midst of life's reality. The hope of the Christian is pinned to the cross of Jesus Christ. It is lived out through our part

126

in the sufferings of him whose resurrection assures us of blessedness.

The Living Word

Our look at parables and beatitudes is meant to alert the reader of the gospels to the truth that the words of Jesus were never, in the early Church, regarded as archive material. It is understood that, as John puts it, his words were 'words of eternal life', words instinct with vitality. Tradition and evangelists re-interpreted and adapted the sayings of Jesus, and even added to them. Nor is this at all surprising, when we appreciate what had come to pass. The Easter experience was the basis of the faith of the apostles, a faith that was centered on the life and words of their Master. Meeting Jesus now as risen Lord they recognized that his words and deeds held a wealth of meaning which had to be drawn out and made available to foster and sustain the faith of others. The Spirit enabled them to understand, in a fresh light, the significance of what Jesus had said and done. The gospels are a record of their understanding.

C. A Word of Exhortation

The epistle to the Hebrews was written to a christian community that had grown sluggish and hard of hearing (5:11; 6:12), that had lost heart (12:12). This explains the tone of the epistle and its repeated exhortations. The readers are first of all called upon to cling to the word of God, as revealed by Christ, lest they stray from the truth (2:1). They must continue on the way perseveringly, like athletes (12:1). They should not be deceived (13:9), nor overcome by weariness (2:3); they ought to resist sin (12:4). On the positive side they must at all times preserve *faith*, in its threefold sense of docile acceptance of the revealed word, of confidence in Providence, and of persevering fidelity to the divine will (3:7; 4:13).

A word of exhortation

The central theme of Hebrews, the priesthood of Christ, is formulated by reference to Jewish theological categories: Christ is superior to angels, to Moses, to the levitical priesthood, and Christ's sacrifice is superior even to the high-priestly liturgy of the Day of Atonement. Such Old Testament concepts were well appreciated by first-century converts though not, even then, by all; inevitably, they lose some of their relevance after twenty centuries. Despite this, we meet throughout the letter religious truths of perennial validity. The author intended his treatise to be 'a word of exhortation' (13:22). The whole is a magnificent statement of the saving work of Christ and constitutes for us today a moving word of exhortation in a time when we may be tempted to 'fall away from the living God' (3:12).

The Son

The prologue (1:1-4) to the epistle announces the great themes to follow: the superiority of the new order of revelation to the old which it replaces; the divinity shared by the Son and manifested to us in him; his place in the cosmos; his role in achieving salvation for us by his passion and return to the heavenly world. In this prologue Christ appears as prophet (1:1), priest (purification from sin) and messianic king (sitting at the right hand of God). He is the expression of God. The Son became an integral part of our human existence and so leads that existence to the place where he now is at God's right hand (2:5-12). Hebrews sees a thorough correspondence between Savior and saved, Son and 'sons', Sanctifier and 'sanctified'. The passage 2:14-18 introduces the central theme: the priesthood of Christ. Jesus is the perfect Mediator because he is true God and true man. Because he has shared completely our human nature he can have compassion for us in our suffering and temptation (chs 1-2).

High Priest

The demands of God's word spoken through Christ are stringent and there is no escaping them (4:12-16). We will be judged on how we may have responded. This might seem to impose an impossible task but there is no need for discouragement. We have confidence in knowing that Jesus is our merciful high priest who will give us all the help we need to be faithful. A high priest is a man officially instituted as mediator between God and men, who represents the cause of men before God, and who offers the gifts of men to God, especially sacrifice for sin. A true priest will be compassionate, showing great benevolence to sinners. Christ was duly called by God and, through his obedience, gained an enriching experience, a practical comprehension of and appreciation of suffering which would enable him fully to sympathize with his brethren (chs 4-5).

The order of Melchizedek

The author intends to prove the superiority of Christ over the Old Testament priests. He begins by showing the excellence of the type of this priesthood, that of Melchizedek, although he soon concentrates wholly on the antitype, Christ. Melchizedek, who appears in the Bible like a meteor (Gen 14:17-20) interests him only as a type of Christ. Three

129

circumstances impress him: the meaning of the names, the conduct of Abraham in regard to the priest-king of Salem, and the silence of Scripture concerning his origin. Melchizedek 'continues a priest forever' because his priesthood, being personal, not subject to the laws of human heredity, and scripturally without beginning or end, enjoys a 'negative' eternity. This priesthood of Melchizedek and Christ is distinguished from all other priesthoods in that it has no human antecedent nor any human succession. The transitory nature of the levitical priesthood is underlined by its suppression; that other priesthood is eternal. Thus, Christ 'is able for all time to save those who draw near to God through him, since he always lives to make intercession for them'. His sacrifice was once-for-all; his priestly work of intercession is unceasing (ch 7).

In his own blood

On the Day of Atonement the Jewish high priest entered the Holy of Holies. Within he sprinkled the blood of animals and on emerging he sprinkled the people. They were thereby 'purified' and were linked again in some manner with God. But all this was only a pale reflection of the reality. Christ, by his death, has entered the Father's presence and from there he sends forth his Spirit, to cleanse us, to renew us, and to create a firm bond between ourselves and God. For Christ mediates a new covenant of friendship between God and mankind, a covenant sealed in his own blood. He does not offer himself again to effect a periodical expiation, like the annual expiation made by the Israelite high priest. Sin has been radically abolished by the unique offering on Calvary (ch 9).

Jesus' death on the cross was the expression of the surrender of his being to the will of the Father: 'Father, into your hands I commit my spirit' (Lk 23:4-6). Then, having poured out his blood for the remission of sins and having entered into heaven to intercede for men, he has become the author and source of a real sanctification and of eternal salvation. The multiplicity of the futile actions of the levitical priests contrasts with the single, permanently effective action of Christ. The sacrifice of Christ has been made once for all, and the forgiveness it achieved has been achieved once for all. This sacrifice of Christ reaches out to succeeding generations of Christians through the sacramental order (10:1-18).

Confidence

One of the features of the letter to the Hebrews is that ever so often, after contemplating some aspect of the mystery of Christ's priestly sacrifice, the author comes down to earth with a practical application. The passage (10:19-25) is a call to confidence in the High Priest: the way to God is Christ himself (cf Jn 14:6). The great truths we believe ought to flow into our daily lives, our relationship with our fellow-Christians. The author shares the expectation, which was general in the early Church, of an early return of Christ ('the Day'). The readers must recall their earlier steadfastness in face of persecution; now, again, there is need for that patient endurance and firm faith. Their fidelity in the past is the best ground of confidence for the future (10:19-39).

Faith

The consistently negative evaluation of the whole levitical system might suggest that the Old Testament has nothing of value for Christians. Not so: there is the inspiring example of the faith of the great men and women of the Old

Testament, with the reminder that faith is necessary for those who move onward to draw near to God. Faith is the firm assurance of the fulfillment of our hope. For, faith is oriented to the future and reaches out to the invisible. Grounded on the word of God, it is a guarantee of heavenly blessedness; it persuades us of the reality of what is not seen as yet and enables us to act upon it (ch 11).

The Pioneer

The realization that the saints of the Old Testament, their noble ancestors in the faith, are witnesses of the great race which Christians must run, will give them heart and encourage them to persevere. Nor are these merely interested onlookers. As in a relay race, the first runners have passed on the baton of faith — they are deeply involved in the outcome of this race of Christians. But the example that is best calculated to sustain the patience and courage of Christians is that of their Lord who was humiliated and crucified only to rise again and enter into his glory. Jesus is the 'pioneer' — that is, chief and leader — offering the example of a faith strong enough to enable him to endure the sufferings of his whole life. 'Looking to Jesus' is the kernel of the letter.

Suffering is part of christian life, a factor of divine pedagogy. When God punishes his children he does so as a Father, for their good. It is a training which will help them towards that holiness of life which will carry them to 'the peaceful fruit of righteousness' (12:11). The author tells his readers: You no longer belong to the old covenant, but to the new. Look no more to Sinai but to the heavenly Jerusalem and its atmosphere of assurance and hope. More than hope, for you already possess the good things of the new

132

economy; you are already citizens of the heavenly Jerusalem. The 'sprinkled blood' of Christ has realized the reconciliation between God and sinful people (ch 12).

The great Shepherd

The letter closes with an exhortation to fraternal charity, by the practice of hospitality and by generosity to prisoners and those suffering ill-treatment. Marriage is worthy of special respect. We today live in a time of rapid change. We are sometimes tempted to ask if there is anything, even within the Church, that will not change. Here we have the answer. Jesus Christ is the same yesterday, today and forever: the same love that led him to die for us on a cross, the same truth that he committed to his Church to teach. Christians are not empty-handed but have something of their own to bring to their celebration of the mystery of the sacrifice of Christ: a liturgy of praise. Unlike the single and unique sacrifice of Christ, this liturgy of praise continues throughout the age of redemption. A closing wish for peace and for progress in virtue reminds the readers that they are in the care of 'our Lord Jesus Christ, the great Shepherd' (ch 13).

D. The Revelation of Jesus Christ

The last book of the New Testament is likely to leave the modern reader perplexed. Its literary form is unfamiliar, its language and imagery bizarre, and its sentiments often bloodthirsty. Yet, it can be so beautiful: '... they have washed their robes and made them white in the blood of the Lamb. ... The Lamb in the midst of the throne will be their shepherd. . .' One does not quite know what to make of this strange mix — which is confidently presented as: 'The revelation of Jesus Christ' (1:1). To bring some order to this

133

complexity and make possible better understanding and appreciation of the book by this 'modern reader', it seemed best to follow the question and answer format below.

INTRODUCTION

Question. The first strange fact about this strange book is its very name — Apocalypse. What does it mean? The short answer is that 'apocalypse' comes from a Greek word meaning 'revelation'. An apocalypse was presented as a revelation, or a series of revelations, made to a seer (one who receives visions). Notice I have said 'an apocalypse'. We have observed that John's strange work is not the only one of its kind — there is the book of Daniel, for instance.

Question. I still do not see why John wrote this kind of work — what was his purpose? The book is addressed to a circle of christian churches in Asia: the western part of modern Turkey. These churches were facing persecution, and the book was written to encourage them: to assure them that Christ was with them; to help them to persevere.

Question. I do not see how those Christians would have been very much encouraged by all the fantastic visions and symbols! *You* would not have been encouraged, because you are a twentieth century citizen of the West. *They* would not have been encouraged if John had presented them with a modern novel. These visions and symbols are part and parcel of the technique of apocalypse as a literary form. John's readers would have been at home with this kind of thing. An example from our own culture may be used to illustrate this. Faced with a legal document, the average layman is quite

134

at sea, because of its peculiar style; an attorney can read it straight off because he is accustomed to the style. John's readers were used to the style of apocalypse. As for symbols— we still use them freely. The shamrock on an Aer Lingus plane tells everyone that it is Irish. A drawing of two children on a road-sign warns us to be careful, that a school is near. And what of the sign of the cross!

Question. But we still have a whole jumble of visions and symbols — is there any basic theme?

Yes, there is — and I think we might put it like this. There is a statement in St. John's gospel, Jesus assuring his disciples: 'In the world you will have tribulation; but have confidence, I have overcome the world'. As stated above, the Apocalypse was written to help Christians faced with persecution. They were only a handful and they were faced with the might of Rome. It must have seemed to them that the world was unmistakably overcoming them. In a way, the book admits as much: it accepts that they will suffer. But it does confidently assure them that, if they are faithful to Christ, they will share his victory. It states quite confidently that he has indeed won the victory as he claimed — but through suffering and death. Revelation makes the very important point that there *is* a christian victory — but one kind of christian victory only: the kind of victory that Christ won.

Question. What would you regard as the highlights of Revelation?

It might be helpful to begin by saying that it is a very important book which has much to contribute. By starting like that, I would imply that a short list of what might be called 'highlights' is necessarily selective.

135

a. First of all, in light of my answer to the previous question, it is a book of *hope*. It declares that evil cannot have the last word; it assures us that, with Christ, we can overcome evil.
b. It tells us a lot of comforting things about our Lord himself: he is the friend who cares, the support of the persecuted, the Lord of joy and peace.
c. There is the interest in the liturgy. Revelation is concerned with the worship of God and Lamb, and the hymns throughout are some of our earliest christian hymns.
d. It is interested in the Church and, indeed, takes a very realistic view of the Church.

CLARIFICATION

Question. You have explained that the book would have been understood by John's first readers. But could you help *me* to understand some of its symbols? For instance, the Four Horsemen?

The famous Four Horsemen of the Apocalypse (6:1-8) provide a vivid and effective description of war and its attendant evils. Like so much else, the idea came to John from the Old Testament (in this case from Zechariah). First, there is a rider on a white horse. In Revelation, white is the color of victory. The rider goes out to conquer. It is the start of war: a leader goes to war. The rider on the red horse stands for the slaughter that is an inevitable feature of war. The third horseman, on a black horse, stands for the famine conditions that follow on war. And the fourth horseman stands for pestilence and disease — another consequence. The four should be taken together as describing war and all the evil it brings in its train.

Question. What about the rider on a white horse who appears later in the book?

Now here is where we need to understand Revelation properly and not in a mechanical way. The only thing these horsemen have in common is the white horse. The rider in chapter 6 (whom I have just described) is a symbol of a king going out to conquer — a symbol of war. But the rider in chapter 19 is Christ — the King of kings and Lord of lords. In that chapter, John is describing Christ's victory over evil and he dramatically presents it as a great battle in which Christ conquers all the followers of Satan.

Question. Then there is 'the Lamb standing as though slain'?

I often wonder why artists will persist in depicting this Lamb lying on the cover of a book! — while it is clearly said that he is standing and reference is to a scroll (5:6-7). Of course, the phrase refers to the death and resurrection of Christ: he, the Lamb, *was* slain, but *is* upright because he has risen from the dead. Incidentally, the description of the Lamb — 'with seven horns and with seven eyes' — warns us how we are to understand such descriptions. 'Horn', in the Old Testament, is a symbol of power; the number seven means fullness — therefore, the fullness of power. The seven eyes stand for his fullness of knowledge; and also the fullness of the Spirit which he gives. This is how we should understand these descriptions. It would be ludicrous to try to paint a picture of a lamb with seven actual horns and eyes! It is the *meaning* of the symbols that matters, and not the details.

Question. The Scarlet Woman and the Beast?

We need to go back a bit and refer to another figure: the great Dragon (ch 12). He is the real villain of the piece — Satan himself. He hates Christ and seeks to destroy his

137

Church. To make war on the Church he uses Rome: the Beast (13:1-10). But there is a second Beast (13:11-18). This is because the problem for the Christians of Asia (for whom Revelation was written) was the worship of the Roman Emperor. He, especially in the East, was regarded as a god, and loyal subjects of Rome were expected to pay him divine honor. This, of course, Christians could not do, and so they were in deep trouble, regarded as disloyal citizens, opposed to the Emperor. If you look at chapter 13 you will see that the whole concern of the second beast is to make men worship the first beast (Rome). And indeed, in Roman eyes, the main value of the cult of the Emperor was that it gave Rome a further hold over its subjects. But to get back to the woman: she is Rome, the city, as the goddess Rome, drunk with the blood of christian martyrs (ch 17). And the beast is the power of Rome; so that woman and beast together equal Rome and its Empire. We should note that this woman stands in contrast to another Woman: the Church (12:1-6).

Question. Then there is also the New Jerusalem?
Yes, that is how the book closes, with a comforting vision (21:9—22:5). In the Old Testament Jerusalem was the city of God. It is very natural that God's heavenly city — let us call it, simply, heaven — should be thought of as a new and perfect Jerusalem. Notice John's description: the length, breadth, and *height* of the city are equal. It is a perfect cube; you just cannot imagine a city like that. John wants to assert that it is perfect. The city walls have twelve gates, each bearing a name of one of the tribes of Israel; it has twelve foundation stones, each bearing the name of one of the apostles of the Lamb. In other words, the heavenly city is the city of the whole people of God: the old Israel and the new. The Temple was the glory of the historical Jerusalem. One

would expect, then, after the glowing description of the city, a particularly striking description of its temple. Instead — and this is a brilliant touch — we learn that there is no temple, nor any need of one: God dwells there, and the Lamb. I have mentioned that other Woman. The images of City and Woman blend and point to the same reality: the holy city, the new Jerusalem, is the Bride of the Lamb.

ASPECTS OF THE MESSAGE

Question. By now we can believe that Revelation has some meaning after all; we can begin to ask what meaning it may have for us, what it can say to us. How would *you* begin?

I feel that, as anywhere in the New Testament, we should begin with Christ. The book conveys something of the oppressive weight pressing on the faith of some first-century Christians. Christ had delivered the world, but the world refuses to be delivered by Christ. His work then seems to be in vain — all because God has given men and women the human freedom to choose against him, as Revelation clearly shows. We have a piercing, sad glimpse into the divine mystery of Jesus. He had said before his ascension that all power on earth and in heaven had been given to him. Where was this power now? These Christians experienced an almost insurmountable contradiction between the truth of their faith and their own daily experience. They felt the absence of Jesus!

Question. The absence of Jesus — that is an interesting point. How is it brought out?

The liturgical hymns of Revelation show that the early Christians did indeed venerate Jesus as the Lord. But (and

139

how sadly reminiscent this is of today's Church) when once their assemblies of the 'breaking of bread' and 'the prayers' had ended, when they had returned to their everyday lives and trials, they saw almost no trace of the glory of Jesus they had sung about. The fact that they had to wait, it seemed, for his second coming was hard enough. But how much harder this waiting was made by their experience of Jesus' spiritual absence then and there. So, we find that, in spite of all the angels and elders and trumpets and thrones, a careful reading shows that the portrait of Jesus is not at all exuberant. It is sober — and this Christ is one of quietude.

Question. All the same, is it very helpful to persecuted Christians — or very helpful to us for that matter — to insist on the absence of Christ?

Of course that would not be helpful, and the book does not insist on it. John precisely wants to show that the Jesus whom they may feel to be absent is very near to his followers, even while they pass through many tribulations. We may see this, perhaps, by looking at some major sections or parts of Revelation.

Question. Before you go any further: what are these parts or sections?

In the first place, the three opening chapters, the letters to the seven churches: Jesus himself speaks to his followers in these churches. After this you find a problem taken up, one very important for the early Christians, the relation of the Church to the former people of God, Israel, in chapters 4-11. Next, in chapters 12-20, the persecution: the Church and pagan Rome. And, finally, the note of triumph after trial, the New Jerusalem, chapters 21-22.

Question. You are saying that each of these parts gives a different aspect or picture of Christ?

Yes. In the letters, Jesus is the one who walks 'amidst the candlesticks' (that is, the churches). He is no absentee land-lord, but knows his people very well indeed. As I said, they *feel* that he is absent. He assures them that he is present and knows all about them — and so you have praise and blame as he deals with them one after the other. Christians can have the assurance of Christ's constant presence and support if they accept the assurance of his love. He is the one who first drew them to the faith they are now asked to keep. It is with love he 'reproves and chastens' because he himself suffers when his followers tolerate idolatry and are Christians only in name. Because he loves his own he cannot endure their indifference, their being 'neither hot nor cold', their lukewarmness. But also because he loves them they have every reason to believe, to hope, to stand with 'patient endurance' — to place unwavering confidence in this love of Jesus at a time when wavering, yielding to imperial commands, would have saved them from immediate trial and pressures.

Question. Is this image of Christ sustained in the rest of the book — the apocalypse proper?

Yes indeed. The Christ of the central section of Revelation (chs 12-20) is he who gives to those who share his sufferings the hope of sharing in his glorious resurrection. Christians have been assured earlier in John's work that Jesus loves them, that he promises to shelter them as the Shepherd who leads them to streams of living water. But there are Christians facing imminent persecution and possible martyrdom: now they need their Lord's word that their very death means a share in their Lord's victory. They need the assurance that their response to a 'call for the endurance and faith of the saints' (14:12) will bring them a share in his resurrection after they have endured to the point of death. Each needs the assurance that, although he be assaulted or martyred by the forces of evil, still he will not have given his life in vain. 'The Lamb *will* conquer . . . for he is Lord of lords and King of kings, and those with him are called and chosen and faithful' (17:14).

Question. A last question: when all is said and done is not the vision of Revelation utopian?

It is important to understand John's notion of history. Revelation banishes any absolute faith in human progress and every blind optimism about historical development. It offers instead the hard reality of how, since the moment of our redemption, the Cross has continued to cast its shadow on the field of history. It has continued to be a symbol of the power of evil and the apparent helplessness of God. Christ as the axis of universal history is a sign of contradiction. His death has awakened not only new life and grace but also powers of disobedience and opposition. The Easter victory did not do away with his mockery, persecution, and crowning with thorns. It is hard to see the Easter Sun still shining in human history. It was with the Cross, towering above history, that the early Church had to associate itself. And we are not understanding Revelation aright if we attempt to escape from this into the perpetual harmony of an Easter glow. History, according to Revelation, is the experience of the Cross. Not to recognize this is to risk not recognizing Jesus himself.

III
THE OLD TESTAMENT

Chapter Seven
The Books of the Old Testament

Our procedure in this section will match that in the foregoing one. Before attempting to evaluate the Old Testament which is the major part of our Bible, it would be sensible to give some idea of what it is, what it contains. In our short presentation we shall look at the main divisions, which will happen, generally, to match the chronological growth of the Old Testament.

The Pentateuch

The religion of the Old Testament, like that of the New Testament, is an historical religion. It is based on the revelation made by God in given times and places and on the interventions of God at certain determined moments. The Pentateuch (meaning 'five-fold' — the books of Genesis, Exodus, Leviticus, Numbers, Deuteronomy: the first five books of our Bible), which traces the history of the first relations of God with his world, and of his election of Israel, is the foundation of the Jewish religion, its sacred book par excellence, its Law. In it the Israelite found the explanation of his own destiny and a way of life. But the Hebrew word *torah*, which we render 'the Law' has a wider

145

signification, one far less juridical, than the English word 'law.' It has rather the sense of 'instruction' given by God to men and women in order to guide their conduct. This is why the whole Pentateuch, not the legislation only, is called the Torah. Framed in a narrative setting which traces the saving plan of God from creation to the death of Moses, the Pentateuch sets out the prescriptions which ruled the moral, social, and religious life of the people. All of these prescriptions — moral, juridical, and cultic — have a religious character, and the whole corpus is presented as the charter of a covenant with Yahweh and is linked with the narrative of happenings in the desert where the covenant was made. This Torah makes known to us the constitution of the people of God and the conditions of the divine choice.

The heart of the Pentateuch

The central plan and the unifying idea of the Pentateuch is summed up in a little credo which the Israelite recited at the ritual offering of the first-fruits:

A wandering Aramean was my father; and he went down into Egypt and sojourned there, few in number; and there he became a nation, great, mighty, and populous. And the Egyptians treated us harshly, and afflicted us, and laid upon us hard bondage. Then we cried to the Lord the God of our fathers, and the Lord heard our voice, and saw our affliction, our toil, and our oppression; and the Lord brought us out of Egypt with a mighty hand and an outstretched arm, with great terror, with signs and wonders; and he brought us into this land, a land flowing with milk and honey. (Dt 26: 5-9).

Here we can learn that God had chosen Abraham and his descendants and had promised them the land of Canaan. Then, when the whole plan seemed to have come to naught in Egyptian bondage, Yahweh intervened again and delivered his people; he made a covenant or pact with them and brought them into the Promised Land. These facts underlie the different traditions; the ultimate structuring of the material into a great synthesis was guided by the very same facts. Hence the Pentateuch, in its basic facts, in the units which variously reflect these facts, and in its final shape, is built around the ideas of election and efficacious intervention and covenant.

The unifying themes of the Pentateuch continue into the rest of the Old Testament, for the Pentateuch is not complete in itself. It tells of the promise but not of its fulfillment and it closes before the entry into the promised land. Even when the conquest is achieved the fulfillment is not yet, for the promise looks ultimately to Christ and to his new covenant.

The Deuteronomical History

The Pentateuch has introduced us to a grouping of writings. And we find that the apparently isolated historical books of the Old Testament do also come in groups. Thus, 1, 2 Chronicles, Ezra, and Nehemiah are so many chapters of one work. Even 1 and 2 Maccabees are (partially) parallel accounts of the same events. The block of writings Joshua to Kings with Deuteronomy as introduction (the 'deuteronomical history') receives special attention in Chapter Nine.

The Prophetical Books

The prophets of Israel fostered and developed a religious tradition which they had inherited. They were guides, specially chosen, along a precarious stage of the spiritual journey that led to Christ. A prophet is a man who has received a divine call to be a messenger and an interpreter of the divine Word. He is a man who has met with God, and who feels himself constrained to speak what, he is convinced, is word of God. His vision of God has penetrated the whole manner of his thought so that he sees things from God's point of view and is convinced that he so sees them.

The prophets are primarily preachers who delivered their oracles and sermons by word of mouth, and that original oral character is still stamped on the written record of their sayings. This means that, by and large, the units which make up the prophetic collections are short and many and take varied forms. Besides, the greater part of Old Testament prophecy is poetic. It has become clear that the oracles and sermons of the prophets were preserved by their disciples and eventually edited by them. In the gradual work of collecting and editing, elements were added. Earlier collections were sometimes broken up and the material was finally arranged according to a plan, sometimes very vague, that must be determined (if possible) for each book. The complex genesis of the prophetical books (or many of them) goes far to explain the disarray that can confuse and exasperate the reader. But their words spring from enduring religious principles. It is up to us to seek out, and apply to our own times, the abiding significance of their message. Prophets were not, and are not, comfortable people. Generally, we want them to go away and leave us alone. We shall look more closely below at a few of these troublers of Israel (pp. 174-183).

The Wisdom Literature

We have stressed the fact that biblical religion is markedly historical and, indeed, the Old Testament bears striking witness to Israel's keen awareness of its unique history. It is all the more surprising, then, to find that in one extensive and important group of writings within this literature (Proverbs, Job, Qoheleth, Sirach, Song of Songs, Book of Wisdom) the historical concern is almost entirely lacking — only the latest of the wisdom books regard the special destiny of the people of God. This is perhaps the main reason why the wisdom literature stands apart from the rest of the Old Testament writings, though the subject matter and the style also mark their distinctiveness. Nevertheless they are an authentic part of the literary and religious legacy of Israel.

Proverbs

In keeping with the accepted notion of wisdom, the maxims of the *Book of Proverbs* are concerned with right conduct. Self-discipline is urged: sobriety in food and drink, control of the tongue. Many of these counsels strike further into the moral order and regard honesty in business, faithfulness in marriage, impartiality in judgment, and the value of almsgiving. At a still deeper level it is recognized and stressed that religious faith is the necessary foundation of the moral life and that man can attain true wisdom only when he is moved by the reverential fear of God. In this the wisdom tradition joins hands with the prophetic and priestly traditions, and Israel's sages would give unhesitating approval to the declaration of Jeremiah: 'Let not the wise man glory in his wisdom . . . but let him who glories glory in this, that he understands and knows me, that I am the Lord who practice kindness, justice, and righteousness in the earth' (Jer 9:23-24).

Retribution

The Torah also plays its part; in particular the deuter-onomic doctrine of reward and punishment is now applied to the individual. While historians had shown the principle at work in Israel's history, the sages contended that the happiness or misery of every man depended on his fidelity to or disregard for Yahweh's law. But the principle had to be applied within the narrow limits of this life — for Israel had no doctrine of a real life after death. Gradually the logic of the facts — the grim reality of life — troubled men and impelled them in sweat and tears, to prepare the ground for a fresh seed, the revelation of an afterlife, with reward and punishment beyond the grave. The authors of *Job* and *Qoheleth* were the two who, courageously, challenged the inadequacy of an entrenched theology. They merit special treatment. (See pp. 184-197).

The Moralist

But the problems which were of such concern to those two did not appear to trouble other sages. Ben Sirach (author of *Sirach* or Ecclesiasticus) did not consider these questions at all (though his book did receive significant additions which did treat of such matters) and is satisfied with the traditional position. His is the practical aim of teaching piety and morality and his book is an important witness to the moral outlook and doctrinal views of Judaism shortly before the Maccabean age, that is to say, in the early second century B.C. The spirituality of the book is grounded in faith in the God of the Covenant, a faith which shows itself in cult and in the practice of justice and mercy. Thus ben Sirach exhorts men to humility, and kindness to the poor. He denounces pride, sins of the tongue, adultery, covetousness, and sloth. The book, in short, abounds in practical religious counsels.

Love

The *Song of Songs* is traditionally classed with the wisdom books. It takes its place in the Bible — at least according to a widely held interpretation of the Song — as the exaltation of human love. In form a collection of love-songs (or an elaborate poem) it is the expression of a state of mind and heart and celebrates the love of a man and a woman — one of the many good gifts of God to mankind (cf Gen 1:31). The book was later re-interpreted in terms of the mutual love of Yahweh and Israel.

The last of the Old

In the most important center of the Diaspora (the numerous Jewish communities 'dispersed' throughout the world of the time), Alexandria, the latest Old Testament writing, the *Book of Wisdom,* appeared. In this cultivated environment educated Jews sought to dress their religion in terms of wider appeal and searched out points of contact between Greek culture and the traditions of Israel. Written in Greek in this environment, Wisdom shows the influence of Greek thought, though the measure of this influence must not be exaggerated. For if the author displays some acquaintance with the various philosophies, this is no more than one would expect from the average cultured Alexandrian. What is most noteworthy is the new teaching, the new hope, which Wisdom emphasizes: 'God created man for immortality' (2:23). After death the faithful soul lives on — not in the shadowy existence of Sheol, but in a life of unending happiness before God (3:9). One thing alone matters: to do God's will and to live in his love, for this is the way to eternal life.

151

The Psalms

The religious poems, which we call the psalms, reflect the ongoing life and faith of Israel. Almost all the psalms may be classified under one of two headings: they are either psalms of praise or psalms of lamentation and petition. There are two ways in which God is praised in these psalms: on the one hand, he is praised for his power and majesty, in the form of a hymn (e.g. Ps 104); and on the other hand he is praised for a specific action which he has just carried out on behalf of the one giving praise (e.g. Ps 30).

Worship and prayer

We may single out three things about the psalms which show them to be not only suitable for contemporary worship but which are also illustrative of a pattern of religious practice which remains valid for today. In the first place, their language is, most often, general and unspecific. Secondly, the psalms grew out of the everyday experience of the people, and this can apply in any age. Then, in the psalms of praise in particular, we see Israel's ability to absorb new experience and adapt new ideas to its understanding of God. This openness to new ideas surely means openness to reinterpretation in a christian context.

Not surprisingly, the Psalter (book of psalms) has become a prayer-book of the christian Church. The first and basic characteristic of prayer in the Psalter is the reality of the divine presence. Another is the association between prayer and life — for one is never more truly alive than when one is involved with the praise of the Lord of life. Then, Israel prayed out of her own tradition, her own history, her own experience. This is a pointer to the realistic basis of our prayer. A fourth characteristic is the imagery of the psalms.

And the question is: Does biblical imagery still have meaning for us, people with a very different culture? In face of abiding interest in the psalms, the answer must surely be yes.

The Chronicler's History

In the third century B.C. a major work, comparable to the deuteronomical history, saw the light. It is distinctive in that it strongly reflects the priestly interests and is dominated by the theological views of its author. This unknown writer is conveniently named the Chronicler — after the title of the first part of his work. A comparison of *Chronicles* with Samuel-Kings carries the conviction that the Chronicler intends to write a history; a closer look at the work gives the further assurance that he has planned to set a religious doctrine in full relief. It becomes clear that, despite a wide material agreement, the outlook and object of the deuteronomical history and of the Chronicler are not the same. In the latter a constant tendency is manifest: to justify from history the solutions which, in the postexilic age (the era after the return of the Jews from captivity at Babylon in the sixth century B.C.), had been given to complex problems, and notably to refer back to David the basic characteristics of the Jewish community. The writer seeks to establish the continuity between the past and the present, and to make the old relevant to the new.

A theology of history

On the whole, this work is more truly a theology of history. The author brings to life again before the eyes of his contemporaries an (idealized) Davidic theocracy. This recalling of the glories of David is designed to make his readers ponder on their vocation as God's people. The story of the restoration (*Ezra, Nehemiah*), coming after the failure of the monarchy, would show how God had remained faithful to his promise. As a new beginning it would turn their hope towards the full establishment of God's kingdom.

The Books of the Maccabees

The first book of Maccabees is the history of the Maccabean uprising to the founding of the Hasmonean dynasty (that is, 175-134 B.C.). The author has been influenced by the style of the deuteronomical history and has been inspired by a similar attitude to the law and its observance, but his work does not attain the stature of the earlier biblical histories. Here there is no evident impact of the prophets. We note instead a step towards a legalism that will eventually become oppressive. Yet, despite its shortcomings, the message of Maccabees is valid and its appeal persists. We are shown what faith and confidence can achieve. And, knowing the aftermath, we are warned that even the best of causes can be betrayed.

The *second book of Maccabees* is not a sequel to the first but deals in part with the same events (176-160 B.C.). Its author is more interested in theology than in history, and in religious standing his book far surpasses 1 Maccabees. An important feature of 2 Maccabees is its confident teaching on the afterlife: the living can pray for the dead and make sin-offerings on their behalf (2 Macc 12:42-45), while the just who have passed beyond the grave intercede for those who still live on earth (15:11-16). The resurrection of the body is taken for granted (cf 7; 14:46). These doctrines are facets of the sure faith and unswerving hope that pervade the book. And they highlight the loving mercy of God and his care for those who are faithful to him.

154

The Writings

In the Hebrew division of the sacred books the third grouping, after the Law and the Prophets, is that of the Writings, books like Esther and Daniel which did not fit into the other two categories. The rubric is designedly vague, and wisely so, because these writings are varied — but all of them would fit our category of fiction. The author of *Ruth* presents, with charm, an idyll of touching family devotion and of country life. We see that the virtues of piety and generosity are rewarded and we clearly discern the guiding hand of divine providence. The milieu in which *Jonah* was written would have been much the same as that of Ruth. It is understandable that, among the handful of returned exiles (from Babylon) a certain exclusiveness had developed. They wished to cut themselves off from contact with others and looked with impatience for God's wrath on the Gentiles. Jonah is a bold declaration that God is God of all peoples. It is no naive tale but a sophisticated satire; and its universalist outlook anticipates that of the gospel. (See pp. 204-206).

A romance

The charming story of *Tobit* has been largely inspired by the patriarchal narratives of Genesis. The book extols family virtues. The older couples, exemplary in their own lives, have brought up their children well. Tobias and Sarah, in their turn, have a lofty ideal of marriage and show themselves keenly aware of their obligations to their parents. Great store is set by generous almsgiving. There is a pervasive atmosphere of faith and trust in God. This charming romance needs no one to plead its cause. (See pp. 206-208).

Deliverance

Baruch, a composite work, in the wisdom tradition, helps us in some measure to discern the secret of the endurance of the communities of the diaspora (scattered Jewish communities): the link with Jerusalem, synagogue prayer, the cult of the Law, rejection of any suggestion of idolatry. The books of *Esther* and *Judith* meet in the common theme of the deliverance of the Jews by the intermediary of a woman and both illustrate the truth that God does not abandon his people, yet the two books are really different in outlook. The former is candidly nationalistic and expresses something of the exasperation of the ghetto mentality. Judith, on the other hand, is universalist in perspective.

Daniel

One of the later writings in the Old Testament is the fascinating book of *Daniel*. It was written in the second century B.C. to encourage the faithful Jews who in the Maccabean rising suffered under and opposed with the sword the religious persecution of Antiochus IV.

The first part of Daniel (chs. 1-6) is a free composition on the basis of earlier biblical texts. This procedure is known by the rather forbidding name of *haggadic midrash* — a Hebrew expression. Midrash, from the verb 'to search out', means a 'searching' of Scripture, an application of a text of Scripture to other times and circumstances. For instance, Dan 9:24-27 is a recasting of a text of Jeremiah (Jer. 25:11-12). The qualification 'haggadic' means that it is a freely composed narrative — a story. The other part of Daniel (chs. 7-12) is apocalypse ('revelation'): in a series of visions it traces the course of history, stressing the ultimate victory of the people of God. Daniel maintains that history is purposeful and moves towards a goal, always under divine control. He tells the story of the past in such a way that the persecuted Jews may understand that their sufferings had a place in God's purpose. The book looks always to the final victory, to the time of the end, to the coming of the kingdom. It sees the messianic age about to dawn, beyond the time of tribulation. God's victory over the forces of evil is assured and those who serve him faithfully will have a glorious part in his triumph.

In prose and in poetry God speaks to us through a literature that is Israel's gift to mankind. Isaiah had declared: 'The word of our God will stand forever' (Is 40:8). And St. Paul assures us that in the pages of the Old Testament we Christians will find encouragement and hope (cf Rom 15:4).

Chapter Eight

The Values of the Old Testament

One may feel that the Old Testament is all very well — but it is just that: *old*. It cannot really be expected to speak meaningfully to Christians. The Old Testament readings in church often do ring strange. Someone has said that the Old Testament is rather like an unwanted guest who can neither be sent away nor entertained properly. It might seem better after all to let it go. Yet, if it is to be true to its heritage, the Church must not only retain the Old Testament but actively use it. For, the Old Testament was authoritative scripture for Jesus himself, who knew no God but its God and who found in it the key to his own person. If perhaps it offends the feelings of some Christians, it did not seem to offend the 'christian' feelings of Jesus.

Promise and fulfillment

One way of seeing the relationship between the Old Testament and the New is in terms of promise and fulfillment. Properly understood, this means that the Old Testament contains the history of the promise which comes to fruition in the New Testament. But Israel's dynamic and historical hope abides, even after its 'fulfillment'. The christian notion of fulfillment should not blot out the Old Testament reality.

And we should respect the lines of continuity *and* discontinuity between the Testaments. If there are discrepancies between different parts within the Old Testament and within the New Testament separately, the situation is compounded when the Testaments are considered as joined. This is an evident human characteristic of the word.

The Old Testament *is* pre-Christian. It was written at a time when Jesus had not yet come and should be understood as such. Jesus is the culmination of God's plan. But this does not mean that he must be the criterion for the meaning and fullness of what God did before he came. We need to do justice to the original setting of the texts, those real situations in Israel which have a value and a meaning of their own. We cannot really consider that Jesus is the 'key' to the Old Testament or that it is understood only in the 'light of Jesus' or the 'light of the New Testament'. The apostles did not first understand Jesus and then turn to the Old Testament. Rather, they turned to the Old Testament in trying to learn to know, understand, and explain him.

If we have in this book taken the New Testament first, that is quite simply because the New Testament is likely to be more familiar to the reader. But now we are seeking to establish the value of the Old Testament. We look directly to itself. And we find that the Old Testament can stand on its own feet. Once we have an understanding of it, we can progress with its line of history and structure of faith ahead to the New Testament. From there we can look backwards and see the Old in a fresh light. Then it will be evident that the Old Testament *is* incomplete. Its salvation history is broken; it never quite arrives at salvation. The entire Old Testament asserts implicitly that Jesus Christ fulfills the redemptive purposes of God which began with Abraham. For all that, the Christian must take the Old Testament

159

seriously — not only as an historical document giving the background of his own faith, but also as of vital importance for life here and now.

God and man

The value of the Old Testament today is not primarily in what it teaches about God, man, and human destiny, but in how it expresses the one abiding value: the meeting between God and man. As the authors of the New Testament could see, the Old Testament's men and events do have an existential value in that they call to imitate God, they summon to decision, they advise conduct to be shunned. The Old Testament also helps us to balance the New Testament's possible impression of a lack of concern with temporal values or concrete needs of everyday life. It manifests a joy in life, while at the same time being realistic in its awareness of pain and mortality. The Old Testament is there to help us to take very seriously a human history which goes on and on and culminates in the total liberation of man.

The limits of the Old

Even the so-called 'limits' of the Old Testament have an educational value: we learn that the limitations of revelation are not set by God, but come from human limitations. Israel's experience of God occurred in history and was subject to the contingency of history. Thus, we can see that the only response which the people could give to its God was that response of which they were capable at each moment of their history. History and culture always conditioned Israel's experience of its God. 'God as lawmaker' is emphasized in the Old Testament, but this is an imperfect human representation of him in our own language.

It was Israel's culture which kept her from finally reaching the christian goal of love of enemies. Such considerations make us more aware that concrete human conditions and cultural limitations do impose limits on man's experience of God and his translation of that experience into action. And, if the limits of the Old Testament are so conceived, then ought not the christian ask himself concerning the limits of the New Testament revelation? Here, too, we are dealing with man's limitations, not God's. The Old Testament has so much to offer — if we are prepared to approach it with reverence and intellectual humility, allowing it to speak for itself.

The ultimate worth of the Old Testament might seem to be the answer to our question asked above: Why is the Bible predominantly Old Testament in extent? It is a partial answer. The full answer is the obvious one. The Old Testament covers more than a millennium of the history and of the religious experience of the people of Israel. And that people never seemed to lack men of religious genius and notable literary gifts, men who were bound to leave clear 'footprints in the sands of time', across the centuries. The New Testament spans, at most, three generations. A marked discrepancy in length between the Testaments is, in the circumstances, what one would expect.

Chapter Nine

The Flavor of the Old Testament

Up to now we have looked mainly at the structure, the bare bones of the Old Testament. One hopes that a closer look at some notable areas of the Old Testament will flesh out the picture a little. And, in lingering over these few writings, we may savour something of the richness of the whole.

A. Inspired Stories

Some of the most familiar biblical stories are those we find in the opening pages of the Bible. Simple, naive stories, or so it would seem. They appear to be the product of an unsophisticated, childlike mind — stories for children by one who is still a child himself. On the contrary, rather like the parables of Jesus, these 'stories' clothe the thought of a great theologian, a man who courageously faces up to a compelling problem.

This problem is the unmistakable presence of evil in the world, of man's sin and his inhumanity, a problem which prompts the question: how can all this have come from a good creator? The answer, given in the story of the Fall, is that man, not God, has brought about the sorry state. Mankind had opened the door to sin and once that door was opened, then, as illustrated in the stories of Cain (Gen 4:1-16)

162

and of Lamech (4:19-24), of the Flood (ch. 6-9) and of Babel (11:1-9), evil entered and spawned. Yet, God did not abandon a sinful mankind: he protected Cain, preserved Noah, called Abraham from the scattered tribes of Babel (12:1-3). With Abraham he would make a new effort to win back the faithless sons of men.

Two traditions

These first eleven chapters of Genesis combine two of the four distinct traditions that make up our Pentateuch: the earliest and the latest — the Yahwistic (10th century) and the Priestly (6th century). The priestly editors (who gave its final shape to the Pentateuch) are manifestly heirs to a long theological tradition. But the Yahwist too (author of the vivid 'stories') is a theologian, a theologian of genius. He has about him something of the deceptive simplicity of John the fourth evangelist: in both of them one is ever discovering some fresh, unsuspected, depth.

While Genesis 1-11, as it stands, is an arrangement of the priestly editors, it is a matter of moment that the lion's share of these chapters goes to the Yahwist. The final editors of the Pentateuch, men of the Jerusalem temple tradition, were trained in a precise scholastic method. Yet the whole Pentateuch — and in particular these eleven chapters — witnesses to their theological broadmindedness. They themselves (in Genesis 1 for instance) carefully avoided the anthropomorphic exuberance of the Yahwist (that is to say, speaking of God in strongly human terms — 'the Lord God walked in the garden in the cool of the day'), but they obviously recognized in his Yahweh their own God and in his faith their own faith. Today we have learned to accept the need for, and the reality of, theological pluralism. It is salutary to reflect that theological pluralism was demonstrably practiced by the priestly editors of Genesis 1-11 and that it is a marked feature of the whole Bible.

God

God stands forth in the opening pages of Genesis as Creator and Savior: a transcendent God who is deeply involved in the world he has shaped. We have reason to be grateful to the magnanimity of the priestly editors. They and the Yahwist have viewed the same God in different focus, and the resulting portrait is so much more rewarding than any they or he could have produced alone. Somehow, we appreciate all the more the complacent declaration that God saw his creation as very good when we match it with the charming picture of Yahweh strolling in the garden at the cool of the day. The loving solicitude of Yahweh for man and his interest in providing him with a helper fit for him gives warmth to the more laconic 'male and female he created them'. In the story of the Flood the grief and anguish of Yahweh and his care to fasten the ark door behind Noah (Gen 7:16) soften the more remote bearing of God in the priestly version of the story.

As it is, we find in these chapters a God in whom we can recognize the Father of our Lord Jesus Christ. He is Creator, Master of all; he is also one who has supreme concern for his creation. Man is his creature, brought forth by his word, yet made in his image and placed over all the works of his hands. We can gaze into the very heart of God, to find great compassion. He is a faithful God, who must be true to himself and punish sin, but who will be faithful, too, to his purpose for man. Even the transcendent God of the priestly tradition is not a remote God. Somehow, we know that he can never distance himself from the creation that has meant so much to him. He will never dwell in splendid isolation. The comforting homely language of the Yahwist serves to bring out more sharply an aspect of God that is always there. He is never the god of the philosophers but a God who meets our human need.

Man

The portrait of man in Genesis 1-11 is paradoxical. There can be no mistaking his place in God's creation, his purpose in God's plan. He is indeed little less than a god (see Psalm 8). But he remains thoroughly and irrevocably human. He was created by God, and ought always to be conscious of his creaturehood. He and the animals are made from a common clay; he like them is enlivened by the breath of God; he like them will return to the ground. He differs not because he has an 'immortal soul' — a concept unknown even to the priestly writers. He is different in his very humanness. He is different as man, because God has made him so. For man is ever a self-transcending being, open to the world around him, reaching out beyond himself to the world in which he lives.

Man is fallen man. And *only* as fallen was man known to the biblical writers. All the more remarkable, then, is their declaration of faith as to his true status. It is the Yahwist again who, unflinchingly, portrays the degradation of man, who limns the disorders of which he is capable. We must ask, in wonder, how Yahweh can tolerate this creature. Even he could 'regret' having made him (Gen 6:6). Not even the radical judgment of the Flood had touched the heart of man (8:21). Yet, this same man, after the Flood, is still the man whom God has made in his own image (9:6). This is the man who meets us in the Gospels, the man of our own experience. If God alone, who created man, can account for the standing of man in creation, it is God alone who can hold out hope to fallen man. 'O God, who created man, and most wonderfully re-created him . . .'.

Man and Woman

When Jesus was to give his authoritative view on the permanence of marriage, he turned to these first chapters of Genesis (Mk 10:2-10). For in these opening pages of the Bible (Genesis 1-3) we find the basis of a rich and positive theology of marriage. It emerges clearly once it is appreciated that these passages present their message in imaginative language and in story. Let us look, briefly, at the relevant texts.

Yahweh God said: 'It is not good for man to be on his own; I will make him a helper fit for him' (Gen 2:18).

This is a striking example of God's solicitude for man. He recognizes that solitude is 'not good' for man; he is determined to provide a 'helper fit for him'. Something more than solitude is involved here: there is helplessness too (see Sirach 36:24-25). Man is to be provided with a helper who will stand alongside him, who will suit him. It is noteworthy that the Hebrew word used (*ezer*), 'helper', 'standby', is normally applied to God himself — as in many of the psalms.

Unity and equality

Because she is God's free gift, man will not participate at the birth of woman: he is plunged into a 'deep sleep'. The 'rib' taken from man is not woman: it is built up into a woman by God's creative power. The rib means the unity and equality of man and woman. Everything here is figurative. And when this new creature stands before his delighted gaze the man breaks into song — the first love-song (Gen 2:23). The underlying story was meant to answer, in popular fashion, the question: Whence this attraction of man and woman, this desire of the sexes for each other? The story gave the answer. Man, who has lost his rib, feels incomplete and will feel so until he gets his 'rib' back, until he finds his woman. Obviously, the woman, too, yearns to find her man from which she, the 'rib', was taken. The biblical writer, however, goes beyond the ancient story and stresses the complementary nature of man and woman in relation to marriage:

> That is why a man leaves his father and his mother and cleaves to his wife, and they become one flesh (2:24).

It is because Yahweh made them for each other from the beginning that man and woman will break all other ties to join in marriage.

Already, the more staid writer of chapter 1 of Genesis has a surprise for us — most uncharacteristically, he breaks into song:

> God created man in his image,
> in the image of God he created him,
> male and female he created them (1:27).

'Man' is created male and female, both of them in the image of God, the two sexes set on equal footing. 'Mankind' finds its full meaning in man and woman together.

> God blessed them and said to them, 'Be fruitful,
>   multiply,
> fill the earth and subdue it; have dominion . . .
>   (Gen 1:26-28).

167

The blessing is not only for fertility but for dominion over the earth; it reaches to all the aspects of human existence. It is a promise for the future, for the responsible and inventive role of man in God's creation. Yet, there is no doubt that the narrative is also more specific and has marriage in view here. It should be noted that the phrase, 'Be fruitful, multiply', is a blessing, not a command. Having created the first man and woman in his image, God — by blessing them — proclaims his intention of carrying on the work begun, in them and in their descendants. It is a task to be achieved by man and woman together.

Woman

The will of the Creator was that woman should be man's helpmate: trusted and respected and loved. It is a woman's *right* to find her true place: to be *as woman* the equal of man. Jesus' declaration on the meaning of Gen 2:24 asserts this. 'What therefore God has joined together, let no man put asunder' is a statement that cuts across a practice of his day based on the accepted inequality of women (divorce as a male prerogative). His own attitude to women shows his constant respect for them as women, his recognition of their true personal value. Where the equality of women is not acknowledged (as in the contemporary christian churches) one can urge in protest the principle of Jesus and the practice of Paul.

Marriage

Alas, the story of man and woman does not end at chapter two of Genesis. After Creation comes the Fall. Yet, that full story gives us an eminently realistic view of sex. It is a creation of God, perfectly good in itself; but it, like every aspect of our humanness, has suffered the consequences of the Fall. However, the state of things created by God has not collapsed hopelessly. Something does remain: an institution within which sexual love is good and where fruitfulness is still a blessing. But that life of perfect happiness, which is the dream of all lovers, is no longer possible: man and woman have been driven from Eden.

That vague memory of Eden is not only a dream of lovers. Creation is not a dream and God's design is not lightly set aside. The first two chapters of Genesis hold up to us the divine plan for mankind. There we can catch a glimpse of our true selves and there, too, we see an ideal of marriage more lofty than our romantic ideal. The rest of the Old Testament shows us sinful man and his struggle to restore some brightness to the tarnished image of God in himself. Finally, God takes a hand and the one perfect image of the Father comes to redeem mankind. But it is men and women who win redemption and in that process marriage, too, is redeemed. It falls within God's saving plan.

B. The Message of History

The reader who has, for the first time, patiently or, perhaps, doggedly, worked through the Books of Kings will understandably feel more than a little confused. He may have accepted that the religion of the Old Testament, just like that of the New Testament, is historical. But surely *this* kind of history has no obvious religious bearing? If he has read further afield he may be excused for failing to find any real link between Joshua-Judges (with 1 Samuel thrown in for good measure) and Kings. But the link is there, and the whole has religious meaning. But one must be able to discern. Then one will come to realize that biblical history is not a hopeless muddle of unrelated events or a mere succession of petty kings and their tiresome squabbles. To the eyes of the biblical historians these details fit, each in its place, into the unified pattern of a great mosaic.

169

The Conscience of a Nation

The king of Assyria invaded all the land and came to Samaria, and for three years he besieged it. In the ninth year of Hoshea, the king of Assyria took Samaria and deported the Israelites to Assyria . . . And this happened because the Israelites had sinned against the Lord their God, who had taken them up out of the land of Egypt, from the power of Pharaoh, king of Egypt, and had adored other gods . . . They built for themselves high places wherever they dwelt . . . they did wicked things, provoking the Lord to anger, and they served idols . . . They despised his laws and the covenant which he had made with their fathers and the warnings which he gave them . . . And they rejected all the commands of the Lord their God . . . Therefore the Lord was very angry with Israel, and removed them out of his sight. The tribe of Judah alone was left (2 Kgs 17:5-7, 9-11, 16-16, 18).

The Lord did not turn from the fierceness of his great anger which was kindled against Judah . . . And the Lord said: 'I will remove Judah also out of my sight, as I have removed Israel, and the Temple of which I said: My Name shall be there.' (2 Kgs 23:26-27).

Judgments such as these are understandable only when we see in true perspective the events that evoked them. The main lines, at least, of Israel's history, up to the end of the monarchy, must be recalled.

Abraham

When in chapter 12 of Genesis Abraham is introduced, we enter a new era; we stand at a decisive moment in religious history. Abraham received a divine command to leave his country and kindred and his father's house and go to a land which the Lord would show him, and he was promised that he would be the ancestor of a great nation. He heard and obeyed and came to the land of Canaan. There he grew old with Sarah his wife. The promise had not been fulfilled and still he put his trust in God, the lifegiver. He had faith in God and in the word of God and found salvation: '"Look at the heavens and, if you can, count the stars". And he said to him: "So shall your posterity be". Abraham believed the Lord, who credited the act to him as justice" '(Gen 15:5-6). Abraham remains for future ages the man of faith, the father of a great nation, the friend of God, recipient of the promise of God. The promise was renewed to his descendants, Isaac and Jacob, and the brilliant career of Joseph seemed to presage its fulfillment. Then followed the hopeless years of slavery in Egypt. Where now was the glorious future promised to the sons of Abraham? Then occurred a mighty event that was to echo through the extent of Israel's history: Yahweh himself intervened.

> When the Egyptians maltreated us and oppressed us and imposed hard labors on us, we cried to the Lord the God of our fathers. The Lord heard our cry and saw our misery, our toil and our oppression, and the Lord brought us out of Egypt with a mighty hand and an outstretched arm, with great terror, with signs and wonders. He brought us into this place and gave us this land, a land flowing with milk and honey (Dt 26:6-9).

Moses and David

Throughout the Old Testament we find that the Exodus is the central event in Israel's memory; the Exodus, though it

171

is the work of Yahweh, immediately conjures up the dominant figure of Moses. He not only led the people from Egypt, but he it was who, afterwards, forged that motley crowd of refugees into a nation and set on foot a mighty religious movement and, further, gave the impetus to the great literary achievement that is the Pentateuch.

After Moses the Israelites were in the land, but they did not yet possess the whole of it; the struggle went on for two centuries. Towards the close of that period the failure of Saul threatened the existence of the nation, but David saved the situation and succeeded in establishing a kingdom and even a modest empire. By that fact, David took his place beside Abraham and Moses: these are the three architects of Israel. Once again there is a divine promise:

> The Lord declares that the Lord will make you a house. When your days are fulfilled and you lie down with your fathers, I will raise up your son after you, who shall come forth from your body, and I will establish his kingdom . . . And your house and your kingdom shall be made sure forever in my presence and your throne shall be established forever (2 Sam 7:11-12, 16).

And yet the historical kingdom of David did not stand. It soon became a divided kingdom. In 721 B.C. Israel fell to the Assyrians and disappeared from history. In 587 Judah fell to Nebuchadnezzar. This must have seemed the end. The house built by Abraham and Moses and David had crashed in ruins. The promise of Yahweh had failed.

A people's failure

For men of faith this was unthinkable. There must be an answer. History provided the answer. Yahweh had not failed;

it was the people who had failed their God. Such, at least, was the verdict of Deuteronomy. This deuteronomical outlook was profoundly religious and striking in its single-mindedness: the nation stood or fell by its fidelity or unfaithfulness to Yahweh and to his Law. This outlook inspired men of faith and vision who not only measured their history by that yardstick but set about editing their traditions, giving, in the process, to that history their own distinctive theological slant. We owe to the deuteronomists not only the present form of the books Joshua-Kings but also our awareness of the significance of their content. For us, no less than for them, it is the meaning of history that matters.

Question and answer

Deuteronomy justifies historically the doctrine of the choice of Israel by Yahweh and outlines the theocratic constitution that is demanded by this divine election. *Joshua* presents the installation of the chosen people in the promised land and *Judges* traces the immediate aftermath, the succession of apostasies and conversions. *Samuel* points out how the theocratic ideal was at last realized under David, after the failure of Saul.

    Kings describes the decline that set in even during the reign of Solomon, and which eventually led to the fall and disappearance of the monarchy. But that sad story of failure is lighted up by hope, by the conviction that the Lord who once led his people out of Egypt 'with a mighty hand and an outstretched arm' can lead them back again from another captivity and set them up again on the ruins of the past. Unfaithfulness was the cause of all the evils which had showered upon them, whereas trust in Yahweh and fidelity to his will are the surety of divine blessings, the blessings that can yet be theirs if they will but turn to their God in truth. This confidence was the cornerstone of post-exilic Judaism, that cradle of the New Testament and of a greater hope.

C. Troublers of Israel

The typical Israelite prophet is a man who has received a divine call to be a messenger and an interpreter of the word of God. He is a man who has met with God. The word which has come to him compels him to speak. 'The Lord has spoken, who can but prophesy?' asks Amos (Am 3:8). Jeremiah, despondent because of his unrelieved message of woe to the people he loved, would stifle the word: 'If I say, "I will not mention him, or speak any more in his name", there is in my heart as it were a burning fire shut up in my bones, and I am weary with holding it in, and I cannot' (Jer 20:9). Not only the words of a prophet but his actions, even his life, are prophecy. The marriage of Hosea is a symbol (Hos 1-3). Isaiah and his children are signs (Is 8:18). Ezekiel multiplies prophetic mimes (Ezek 4:3; 12:6, 11; 24:24). Whatever the form of the message, the prophet's vision of God had permeated the manner of his thought so that he saw things from God's point of view, and was convinced that he so saw them.

Armed with this conviction, the prophet was outspoken, a merciless critic of the people and of the establishment. Each of the great prophets richly deserved the epithet petulantly branded by Ahab on Elijah: 'troubler of Israel' (1 Kg 18:17). The prophets were not comfortable people to have around. But the world of Israel, and our world too, is so much the richer because of them. Here we shall consider only three of an impressive band.

174

Amos

Amos was the great champion of justice, who vindicated the moral order established by God and enshrined in the covenant. He castigated the disorders that prevailed in an era of hectic prosperity (the reign of Jeroboam in Israel — 783-743 B.C.). To his eyes, the symptoms of social decay were glaring. Wealth, concentrated in the hands of a few, and these the leaders of the people, had corrupted its possessors; oppression of the poor was rife; the richly-endowed national religion, with its elaborate ritual, provided a comfortable, self-righteous atmosphere. It was this dangerous complacency that the prophet set out to shatter.

Privilege and obligation

The series of oracles (Am 1:2 — 2:16) shows how dramatically he could accomplish this. The people listened, doubtless with approval, to the threatened punishment of God on six neighboring nations: Damascus, Gaza, Tyre, Edom, Ammon, and Moab. Then comes the climax, the seventh oracle (the oracle against Judah — Am 2:4-5 — is a later addition), and out of the blue the prophet's thunderbolt strikes Israel! Yahweh is clearly shown to be master of all peoples (cf 9:7), but he has chosen one people: the whole family which he brought up out of Egypt (3:1). With the privilege of that choice goes a corresponding obligation: 'You only have I known of all the families of the earth, therefore I will punish you for all your iniquities' (3:2). Israel has received more, and of her more will be required; divine justice demands it.

175

Conversion

Amos saw that nothing short of a radical change of life could save Israel (5:4-6, 14-15) and he feared that it would not come. He warned those who looked to the 'Day of the Lord' as the time of the triumph of God's people over all its enemies that the Day would be darkness and not light (2:18). He saw that the slumbering Assyrian giant would soon waken and destroy Israel (3:9-11). There was only one way to avert the wrath to come: 'Hate evil, and love good, and establish justice in the gate; it may be that the Lord, the God of hosts, will be gracious to the remnant of Joseph' (5:15).

Amos did not speak in riddles; his message was uncompromising and unmistakable. We are left in no doubt that this was so for, in a revealing passage, we are shown an indignant Amaziah, priest of the Israelite sanctuary of Bethel, sending this troublesome Judean interloper packing: he had had the effrontery to speak against king Jeroboam in the king's own sanctuary. But Amos took care to have the last word — a word that could bring no comfort to Amaziah or to his royal master (7:10-17). And the true prophet has a disconcerting propensity to be right.

Jeremiah

Jeremiah, of all the prophets, is best known to us as an individual. His book contains many passages of personal confession and autobiography, as well as lengthy sections of biography. He stands out as a lonely, tragic figure whose mission seemed to have failed. Yet, that 'failure' was his triumph as later ages were to acknowledge.

176

The diary of a soul

It is possible to trace the spiritual progress of Jeremiah and to see in him the purifying and strengthening effect of suffering, for the most impressive message of the prophet is his own life. He was a man of rare sensitivity with an exceptional capacity for affection — and his mission was 'to pluck up and to break down, to destroy and to overthrow' (1:10) and to cry out, without respite, 'violence and destruction' against the people he loved (20:8). We find in him, to a marked degree, personal involvement (4:19), a feeling of solidarity with the people in their tribulation (8:19-23), and even with the land itself in its devastation (4:23-26). The *Confessions* are central for an understanding of Jeremiah (11:18 — 12:6; 15:10-21; 17:12-18; 18:18-23; 20:7-18). They are a record of his communing with his God and were surely never meant for public proclamation. Not only are they fascinating because they permit us to gaze into the heart of a prophet; they are also encouraging because they let us see how very human the prophet is. Jeremiah had never really wanted to be a prophet (1:6; 17:16; 20:7-9) and he continued to discuss the trials of his office with Yahweh throughout his life. He was overwhelmed by the sheer burden, the humanly impossible demand of his task; his prayer is the prayer of Gethsemane.

The relevance of Jeremiah

Jeremiah has particular relevance for our day. His predecessors, as far as we know, accepted their prophetic mission with submissiveness — Isaiah indeed with eagerness (Is 6:9). But Jeremiah had to question and to understand; there is in him even a certain rebellion against decrees of the divine will. And he was not at all satisfied to accept, uncritically,

177

traditional theological positions. He struggled, as the author of Job was to do centuries later, with the problem of retribution (12:1) and asserted the principle of individual (as against collective) responsibility (31:29-30). But, mostly, it was his own prophetic office that was his burden, and it was indeed a burden far heavier and more painful than that of any other prophet. He needed, all the more, the support of his God. His obedience was so much the greater because of his questioning, because he felt its yoke, because it led to a feeling of abandonment. It is God's secret why he asked the most faithful of his ambassadors to walk this dark road.

The sufferings of the prophet are described with a grim realism that recalls the description of the Passion. There are no miracles here, no legion of angels: Jeremiah is abandoned to his enemies and is powerless. And he makes no impression on them. It is not surprising that Christians have seen him as a type of Christ. Jeremiah's clashes with his prophetical colleagues (those whom we would term the 'false prophets') were probably among his hardest battles. We can gather this from his tract against the prophets (23:9-40) and from his dramatic encounter with Hananiah (ch. 28). His message was entirely different from that of his colleagues.

The new covenant

Jeremiah's calm conviction that faithless Jerusalem would fall is found, among other places, in his letter to those exiled to Babylon in 598 (29:16-20). Yet, in the same context, he can frame a promise: 'For I know the plans I have for you, says the Lord, plans for welfare and not for evil, to give you a future and a hope' (29:11). This hope is held out not to those left in Jerusalem, but to the exiles — a point of view more explicitly expressed in the vision of the two baskets of figs

(24:5-7). Thus there is the remarkable factor that the same Jeremiah, who so pitilessly demolished false hope, put before his people a positive hope for the future. His efforts to bring his people to their senses had failed, but it is the greatness of the man, and the grandeur of his faith, that precisely during the most tragic moment of his life he spoke his optimistic oracles, notably those of chapters 30-33. He saw that the old covenant would be replaced by a new one (31:31-34) when God would act directly on the heart of man, when he would write his law on that heart, and when all men would know Yahweh.

What is new about the covenant is not the *torah* (the 'instruction', 'guide of life') which it enshrines. The revelation at Sinai is not to be cancelled; a covenant given by Yahweh cannot be cancelled or taken back. The covenant itself was not inadequate — it was the people who had failed. What is new is that there is a change in the way in which the divine will is to be conveyed to men. Yahweh is to by-pass the process of speaking and listening, and put his will straight into Israel's heart, and Israel will hear and obey perfectly. Jeremiah's own experience is reflected here: he had preached to a hopelessly obdurate people; he is convinced that God must take a hand and change the heart of man (cf 32:37-41). He glimpses the era of the Spirit as St. Paul will describe it — the 'law of the spirit of life' (Rom 8:2); he beholds the new man led by the Spirit, moved from within.

The greatest tribute to Jeremiah was paid by the one whose way he had prepared. On that night before the Lord went to his death, he brought the most solemn promise of the prophet to fulfillment: 'This cup is the new covenant in my blood' (Lk 22:20). God had set his seal on the life and message of his servant.

179

Ezekiel

During the first part of his ministry Ezekiel's was very like that of Jeremiah. It might be summarized like this:

> The people of Israel are gravely culpable. God is just and is preparing to punish them. Very soon the siege of Jerusalem and the great deportation will show what an intervention of Yahweh means.

In one respect Ezekiel differs notably from Isaiah and Jeremiah: when he speaks of sin he has not in mind transgressions of the social and moral commandments, but liturgical offenses. For him, the cause of Israel's approaching fall lay in a failure in the sphere of the holy. She had defiled the sanctuary (5:11), turned aside to other cults (8:7-18), and taken idols into her heart (14:3-11); in a word, she had 'rendered herself unclean' in the sight of Yahweh. The great allegories of chapters 16 and 23 and the historical retrospect of chapter 20 are emphatic on this score. There can be no mistaking the priestly point of view. Though truly a prophet, Ezekiel's roots are in the tradition of the priesthood; and so, the standards by which he measures Israel's conduct are the 'ordinances' and the 'judgments' which Yahweh gave to his people (5:6; 18:5-9; 33:25). The priestly tradition colored his preaching, and his great vision of the future (40-48) is aptly called the Torah of Ezekiel.

The nation

The three historical reviews (chs 16; 20; 23) hold not only liturgical interest; they occupy a special place in Israel's conception of her history. True, the allegories are lengthy and repetitious, and the language is consciously crude. Ezekiel seems to wish to say all that can be said about Israel's

180

unfaithfulness, her indifference to the love of God, and her utter failure to obey. The picture he paints could scarcely be blacker than it is. But we need to keep in mind that he is justifying the divine judgment which is to come about in the near future: even the divine patience has at last run out. We also need to observe that the prophet points to God's saving will — now more than ever seen to be free and unmerited (cf 16:60-63; 20:40-44). In this sense, the three somber chapters are the prelude to the glory of Yahweh's act, for it is evident that his salvation cannot be based on any good in Israel herself.

The individual

Ezekiel is concerned not only with the nation but with the individual too. At this time the old conception of a man's guilt being incurred by his whole family, especially by his children who had to answer for it, was proving inadequate (cf Jer 31:29; Ezek 18:2). The celebrated vision of the sins of Jerusalem (Ezek 8-11) provided Ezekiel with the elements of the solution; he developed these and proclaimed the moral principles in chapter 18 (cf ch. 35). From these principles a fundamental religious truth, belief in retribution after death, will one day be deduced — but that day is centuries later. In the meantime, the prophet showed himself the great champion of individual responsibility. True, this idea was not absent from Yahwism before his time; it was present, vaguely at least, from the beginning, but now it receives powerful expression:

> The soul that sins shall die. The son shall not be responsible for the iniquity of the father, neither shall the father be responsible for the iniquity of the son; the righteousness of the righteous shall be his alone, and the wickedness of the wicked shall be his alone (18:20).

181

The sentinel

Ezekiel was called to be a 'watcher' for the house of Israel, a pastor of his people (33:1-9). He had not only to deliver the divine 'word' of prophecy; he was also like a sentinel on the city wall who would warn the people of approaching danger, who would give Israel a chance to 'turn', to repent. He saw his pastoral office as not just an extension of his prophetic calling; rather, it became his duty to live for other people, to seek them out and to place himself at their disposal. His words were designed to give comfort and hope to the individual and to demonstrate that Yahweh desires only repentance and obedience. When the heaviness of divine judgment brings his exiled people to the verge of despair, he faces the problem squarely. He faces the alternatives of life and death: man lives by righteousness, he dies through sin. Man is free to choose between the two and the open door to the choice is repentance (33:10-20). The exiles are to live by Yahweh's word — he will perform his promised works (12:24-25). It is Ezekiel's pastoral concern to help his people to see themselves as they really are and to know their God as he truly is. Then right relations will be restored and he will be their God in earnest, and they will be his people indeed.

The good shepherd

Ezekiel had a sublime vision of the majesty of God, one notably influenced by the priestly tradition to which the prophet is heir. Yahweh is exalted above all creation, enthroned in majesty above his universe; no words can describe him. He is the holy one, transcendent, rather remote; hence the prophet's insistence on a worthy liturgy. Yet, at the same time, he sees this God as the redeemer. In a moving chapter (34) Yahweh is portrayed as the good shepherd who cares for his sheep, who performs the functions of the righteous ruler, who searches for the lost in dark ravines, and who finds for them fresh pasture. That is why Ezekiel's call for a sincere conversion to Yahweh, for a new heart and a new spirit, points to a personal God, a God who is intensely present. His insistence on the need of interior religion indicates a personal relationship to God which, if not as movingly expressed as it is by Jeremiah, is nonetheless very real.

New heart, new spirit

In the promise of a new heart and a new spirit (36:23-28) the prophet echoes Jer 31:31-34. Here, too, the purpose of God's saving activity is the re-creation of a people capable of obeying the commandment perfectly. 'A new heart I will give you, and a new spirit I will put within you; and I will take out of your flesh the heart of stone and give you a heart of flesh' (Ezek 36:26). Thus equipped with a new heart and the bestowal of the spirit, Israel will be able to walk in the path of the divine ordinances. The promise of salvation is prefaced by the words: 'It is not for your sake, O house of Israel, that I am about to act, but for the sake of my holy name' (36:22). This is a recurring thought: that by gathering Israel and bringing her back to her own land, Yahweh manifests his holiness in the sight of the nations (20:41; 28:25; 36:23). Israel, by her infidelity, had profaned the name of her God before the nations; now God owes it to his honor that the covenant should be re-established. But there is more to it than that. Many of the predictions of coming events conclude with the words: 'that they may know that I am Yahweh'. The final goal of divine activity is that Yahweh should be recognized and worshiped by those who have never known him, or who do not know him as he is.

D. A Pair of Rebels

In the varied wisdom literature of the Bible two books stand apart: *Job* and *Qoheleth* (Ecclesiastes). Their authors are theological rebels, taking a firm stand against a position that otherwise went unquestioned. Theirs was the not uncommon fate of such courageous questioners — to be ignored in their own day. But time was to vindicate the truth of their perception. And they are congenial figures in the adventurous theological climate of our day.

THE BOOK OF JOB

The Book of Job belongs to the stage when the idea of individual retribution in this life palpably ran up against insoluble practical difficulties. For an understanding not only of this book but of the great bulk of the wisdom literature, it is important to have in mind that the Hebrews had a very vague notion of the afterlife. At death a man did not quite disappear, he continued to exist in some dim, undefined way in Sheol; but in that dismal abode of the dead all, rich and poor, good and bad, were equal. Given this situation, it is inevitable that, throughout most of the Old Testament, retribution of good or evil was seen in an exclusively earthly perspective, strictly within the confines of this life. It was not until the first half of the second century B.C. — a good two centuries later than the book of Job — that the doctrine of retribution after death made its appearance (cf Dan 12:2). Until that point was reached, it had to be (if there be justice at all) that both good and wicked must find their just deserts *here on earth*, and the received theology stoutly maintained that such was indeed the case. But progress was made by troubled souls (cf Ezek 18:2; Jer 31:29; Mal 2;17) searching for a solution that was truly the measure of reality. The Book of Job marks the longest stride in that progress.

184

The patience of Job?

Job has become a figure of proverbial patience, but anyone who has troubled to read the Book of Job may well be at a loss to understand how he came to win such a reputation. After all, he curses the day of his birth in no uncertain terms, and more than once he practically serves God an ultimatum. But what if there are two Jobs! This, indeed, is more or less the case. The author of the book found his inspiration in a story about a legendary Edomite sheik who, when tried by Satan — not yet the evil spirit of later biblical tradition — proved unshakably faithful. On the basis of this story Israel's greatest poet built his masterpiece.

The prose sections (Prologue and Epilogue, 1:1-2:13; 42:7-17) no doubt do reflect a popular story — but one that has been rewritten by the author of Job. And that story, naive though it may seem, is an essential part of the work. Indeed, it is vitally important for an understanding of *Job*. Job protests his innocence, while his friends are convinced of his sinfulness. Who is in the right, they or he? Without the Prologue we would have no means of knowing. But this prologue puts the reader in the picture. The trials of Job follow on a wager between God and Satan. Twice (1:8; 2:3) God acknowledges the righteousness of 'my servant Job'; twice Job's steadfastness is asserted (1:22; 2:10). And the epilogue, with its description of the restoration of Job's fortunes, is a vindication of his righteousness. The reader is left in no doubt.

The Problem of Job

In the dialogues Job wrestles with a tormenting problem: he is suffering, yet knows himself to be innocent. The inadequacy of the traditional position (the traditional doctrine of retribution, in its simplest form, is that the good are rewarded and the wicked are punished *in this life*) has become apparent, but men can close their eyes to a disturbing new truth. Here the three friends are the champions of 'orthodoxy'; they have accepted the classic teaching without question and quite refuse to admit that it will not fit the facts of the present case. Their position is very simple: suffering is punishment for sin; if a man suffers it is because he is a sinner — the facts must be made to fit the traditional viewpoint! Hence they proceed to comfort the sufferer by pointing out that he must be a sinner — and a great sinner at that, judging by his sufferings — and they grow more insistent as he protests his innocence.

Conservatives and progressives

The author has brilliantly sustained the contrast between two irreconcilable theological positions. Indeed, he has shown how Job and his friends drift further apart. And, perhaps not without malice, he shows that while they become more and more sure of themselves, Job becomes more and more open to God. In particular, the way of Eliphaz, the senior of the comforters, is a satirical comment on theological intransigence. At first, Eliphaz, serene in theological rectitude, is the soul of benignity towards the benighted Job. And he is sure that the sufferer will — must — listen to sweet reason. Job is being rightfully punished for his sin; but let him take heart:

> Behold, happy is the man whom God reproves;
> therefore despise not the chastening of the almighty
> (5:17).

He has no doubt as to the lot of a repentant Job:

> You shall come to your grave in ripe old age (5:26).

186

In the second discourse Eliphaz is petulant. Really, this is too much: Job has dared to question the wisdom of his friends, he has challenged their theology. Who does he think he is indeed:

> What do you know that we do not know?
> What do you understand that is not clear to us? (16:9).

However, Eliphaz is still determined to help, to show Job the error of his ways:

> I will show you, hear me;
> And what I have seen I will declare (15:17).

But Job will not be taught. He still dares to protest his innocence, still will not acknowledge the 'truth'. For Eliphaz *knows* that he is right: his theology tells him so. With hair-raising self-assurance he not only insists on Job's guilt, but cooly examines Job's conscience for him, cataloging his crimes: he is a usurer and an exploiter of the poor, a man insensitive to the misery of others (22:5-11). Eliphaz, we know, will remain unmoved by Job's vehement rebuttal of his charges (ch. 31). It matters not at all that Job *is* innocent in God's sight: by the standard of a man's theology he is clearly in the wrong.

But Job does protest and continues to protest. He *knows* that he is innocent; at least he is certain that he has done nothing to deserve such trials. His world has broken in pieces about him for he too had subscribed to the traditional doctrine. Now he sees that it does not meet his case — but he has no other solution. He struggles manfully with his problem, but there is no outlet; his sufferings are now utterly meaningless and he is tempted to question the justice of God.

> How long wilt thou not look away from me,
> nor let me alone till I swallow my spittle? (7:19).

> Behold, he will slay me; I have no hope;
> yet I will defend my ways to his face (13:15).
>
> He has kindled his wrath against me,
> and counts me as his adversary (19:11).

The darkness of faith

This Job is not the improbable hero of the older tale, but a man of flesh and blood, striving to find a glimmer of meaning in the inscrutable ways of God, a man groping in thick darkness — but it is the darkness of faith. The grandeur of Job is that he can 'defy the sufferings which overwhelm him to rob him of his faith in a hidden God'. In his agony he may have criticized God and his ways, but this is balanced by his cry for God and his yearning to meet him:

> I would speak to the Almighty,
> and I desire to argue my case with God (13:3).
>
> Behold, I go forward, but he is not there;
> and backward, but I cannot perceive him;
> on the left hand I seek him, but I cannot behold him;
> I turn to the right hand, but I cannot see him.
>
> But he knows the way that I take;
> When he has tried me, I shall come forth as gold (23:8-
> 10).

And, fittingly, in the climax, God does speak to Job (chs 38-39; 40:6 — 41:34). Then, overwhelmed by the marvels of God's works, he makes his final profession of faith and his submission:

> I had heard of thee by the hearing of the ear,
> But now my eyes have seen thee;
> Therefore I despise myself,
> and repent in dust and ashes (42:5-6).

Yet, though he speaks of having seen God, the mystery remains, for Job has no knowledge of retribution beyond the grave. God's ways towards him are still inscrutable. But if, theoretically, the problem looms as largely as ever, he has solved it as a practical issue: he has come to accept God as he is and he no longer questions the divine purpose. Hence, though we have shattered the stained-glass Job — the inhumanly patient man — we have raised instead the real Job, the man of faith. And from him we can learn that faith in a God whose ways we cannot know does lead to patience and to peace.

Compromise

The Book of Job was too potent to be taken neat; a later editor tried his hand at watering it down. It would seem that this concern accounts for the rearrangement of chs. 22-27. The editor's main contribution is in the Elihu speeches (chs 32-37). He had felt, not unreasonably, that the author had not done justice to the traditional doctrine and his Elihu makes a somewhat better case than any of the comforters. But even he fights a lost cause and, in the end, he too has to point to the work of God (36:24 — 37:24). In God alone is the answer to Job's problem.

THE BOOK OF QOHELETH

The Book of Qoheleth (Ecclesiastes) comes after Job and marks a further development in biblical thought. Once again the problem of personal retribution is taken up, and once again the traditional doctrine is found wanting. This is not to say that the position of Job is just restated in more emphatic terms — it is not at all a parallel treatment of the matter. Job was able to show that suffering does not presuppose sin in the sufferer and can be quite independent of guilt;

but what about the reward of the virtuous man? It is precisely this other side of the picture, the view that the just man must be happy, that Qoheleth questions. He observes that when a man, even a righteous man, has all he wants, he is not content. Now, at last, the inadequacy of the accepted position has been well and truly challenged, but the time is not yet ripe for the step that will enable theologians to come forward with the final, satisfactory solution. In the meantime, even so gifted a sage as ben Sirach will still take the 'orthodox' view for granted. Qoheleth is of very different cast: he refuses to take a mechanical view of Providence. For him God is no accountant keeping a rigid balance sheet and doling out life and death, happiness and misery, in strict proportion to man's virtue or guilt. God is in no way answerable to man.

The Book

'Ecclesiastes', the name by which the book is usually known, derives by way of the Vulgate from the Greek *Ekklēsiastēs*. It is a rendering of the Hebrew *Qoheleth* a word which describes 'one who speaks to an assembly', that is, a speaker or preacher. Thus Qoheleth (Ecclesiastes) is not a proper name but the designation of a function.

The title (1:1) identifies Qoheleth with Solomon (cf 1:12, 16; 2:4-10), but this is no more than a literary convention, since many of the wisdom books are similarly attributed to the wise king. Most scholars agree that Qoheleth comes, chronologically, between Job and Sirach. The book is influenced by Greek culture, though not in any fundamental way. Its era is that of Ptolemaic dominance and hence of close contact with Egypt — not the Egypt of the ancient sages but an Egypt very much hellenized. The atmosphere of hellenism was all around; the author could not escape it. But the most we may legitimately say is that Qoheleth, while remaining essentially Israelitic in outlook, does mark a step towards Greek thought.

'Cast a cold eye'

Qoheleth casts a cold eye on human life, and he does not flinch from what he sees there. He has the courage to admit that the things which are supposed to satisfy man do not satisfy him. He tests our customary values and finds them wanting.

Test of pleasure (2:1-11)

'I said of laughter, "It is mad," and of pleasure, "What use is it?"' This is the disillusion of one who has everything. It is an ailment of our affluent society.

Test of wisdom (2:12-17)

Fulfillment is not to be found in pondering on the meaning of life. It is true that wisdom excels folly as light excels darkness. The wise man walks with wide-open eyes, while the fool stumbles in the dark. Yet, there is the irony of the situation: the wise men dies just as readily as the fool.

Test of work (2:18-23)

One must, inevitably, leave the fruit of one's toil to another — and whether he be a wise man or a fool, one cannot really know.

Test of Theology

No more than it does Job, does the traditional theology of retribution satisfy Qoheleth: he unmasks its inadequacy:

> I saw under the sun that in the place of justice, even there was wickedness, and in the place of righteousness, even there was wickedness (3:16).

> If a man begets a hundred children, and lives many years, so that the days of his years are many, but he does not enjoy life's good things . . . I say that an untimely birth is better off than he (6:3).

> In my vain life I have seen everything; there is a righteous man who perishes in his righteousness, and there is a wicked man who prolongs his life in his evil-doing (7:15).

> There is a vanity which takes place on earth, that there are righteous men to whom it happens according to the deeds of the wicked, and there are wicked men to whom it happens according to the deeds of the righteous. I said that this also is vanity (8:14).

None of this is very comforting — except for the comfort of realism. But how much more refreshing is it than an attitude that will not face reality:

> I was young and now I am old,
> but I have never seen the just man forsaken
> nor his children begging for bread (Ps 37:25).

This is pathetic: a desperate clinging to a doctrinaire position in face of the evidence. Surely, one must prefer the honest candor of Qoheleth. And he has the courage of his conviction: he throws down the gauntlet to his peers, questioning their academic stance:

> When I applied my mind to know wisdom ... then I saw all the work of God, that man cannot find out the work that is done under the sun. However much man may toil in his seeking, he will not find it out; even though a wise man claims to know, he cannot find it out (8:16-17).

Such bluntness cannot have won him popularity. This is wryly admitted by the editor (responsible for the Epilogue, 12:9-14): 'The sayings of the wise are like goads' (12:11). He wonders aloud whether it might have been better if such an uncomfortable book had not been written: 'Of making many books there is no end' (12:12).

Life

If everything in life is vanity, then life itself is a riddle. The after-life cannot offer its solution to the riddle, because there is no after-life. The problem of existence must be answered within the brief span between life and death. Here, too, Qoheleth is the realist. Life is not, or is not always, full of pain, a cruel joke. If there is vanity and pain there is also meaning and joy. One must thankfully take the smooth with the rough:

> In the day of prosperity be joyful, and in the day of adversity consider; God has made the one as well as the other (7:14).

One must count one's blessings. This is all the more important when one cannot lift one's gaze beyond the horizons of this life. The apparently hedonistic recommendations of

Qoheleth are nothing other than a thorough-going acceptance of the essential goodness of God's creation:

> There is nothing better for a man than that he should
> eat and drink and find enjoyment in his toil. This also,
> I saw, is from the hand of God (2:24).

Life is short, and too precious to be wasted; we have only
one life and we should make the most of it:

> Whatever your heart finds to do, do it with your might:
> for there is no work or thought or knowledge or wisdom
> in Sheol, to which you are going (9:10).

And life is precious, so precious in contrast to the meaning-
lessness of death:

> He who is joined with all the living has hope, for a
> living dog is better than a dead lion. For the living
> know that they will die, but the dead know nothing
> (9:4-5).

Death

It is obvious that the problem of death — the most universal
human experience — hangs like a dark shadow over the
whole book. Life ends in death — whether life be a tissue of
pain or one with its measure of fulfillment. This is the ultimate vanity. Qoheleth describes death in terms of Gen 2:7 —
'The dust returns to the earth as it was, and the spirit returns
to God who gave it' (12:7). Man is effectively dissolved.
Indeed, Qoheleth can find no distinction between man and
beast in this respect:

> For the fate of the sons of men and the fate of beasts is
> the same; as one dies, so dies the other. They all have
> the same breath, and man has no advantage over the

194

beasts for all is vanity. All go to one place; all are from dust, and all turn to dust again. Who knows whether the spirit of man goes upward and the spirit of the beast goes down to the earth? (3:19-21).

The point he makes — and how effectively he makes it — is that death is the great leveller. He is thoroughly biblical in his conviction that man is the summit of God's creation, standing apart from and above all other creatures (Gen 1-2). And yet there is the inescapable fact that man and beast meet in death. Let us recall that Sheol is a place of darkness and gloom, away from the sight of God. In this perspective we can gauge the grandeur of the faith of Qoheleth. He has looked on life and death and he has had the honesty to acknowledge that, from a human point of view, both the one and the other are vanity. But his faith reaches beyond human confines to God, and like Job, in God he finds the answer to his problem.

Faith

Qoheleth has had the courage to question and to challenge because his vantage point is one of faith. He questions not because he doubts but because faith is a way through darkness; man cannot know the work of God. And, at the end of all, Qoheleth is content to acknowledge that, because God *is* in his heaven, all is well with the world. He is content to leave everything in the hands of his God:

> I know that whatever God does endures forever; nothing can be added to it, nor anything taken from it (3:14).

Man must accept that God's ways are not our ways:

> Consider the works of God; who can make straight what he has made crooked? (7:13).

195

All that God has made is good, the whole of creation (though so much is riddlesome to man) has a marvelous purposefulness:

> He has made everything beautiful in its time (3:11).

If man is to make the most of life, to grasp thankfully whatever joy comes his way, that is the gift of a benevolent God:

> Everyone to whom God has given wealth and possessions and power to enjoy them, and to accept his lot and find enjoyment in his toil — this is the gift of God (5:19).

This can be put more forcefully:

> It is God's gift to man that every one should eat and drink and take pleasure in all his toil (3:13).

Here is indeed the Creator who had looked with complacency upon his creation and had entrusted this earth to man for his benefit; the God who bears patiently with an ungrateful and rebellious mankind.

The most important thing in life is to stand right with God; this is the strong conviction of Qoheleth:

> I know that it will be well with those who fear God, because they fear before him (8:12).

He can display an extraordinary optimism:

> Go, eat your bread with enjoyment, and drink your wine with a merry heart; for God has already approved what you do (9:7).

196

But, in true biblical fashion, the transcendence of God is taken for granted:

> Be not rash with your mouth, nor let your heart be hasty to utter a word before God, for God is in heaven and you upon earth; therefore let your words be few (5:2).

Throughout, Qoheleth is the supreme realist. And in the last analysis, he is something more. He has plunged more deeply yet into the dark labyrinth uncovered by Job, and he too, despite his vain searchings for an outlet, clings desperately to his faith in God. No more than Job does he solve his problem, but he has cleared the way by contesting illusory solutions and by forcing men to face up to the true state of affairs. His is a providential role. Qoheleth did not reach the threshold of the gospel. But it is true to say that before one can understand "Blessed are the poor" it was first necessary to have recognized that "Blessed are the rich" is not true . Qoheleth challenged his contemporaries to think. He did not provide answers, but he raised questions which, some day or other, had to be faced.

IV
READING THE BIBLE

Chapter Ten

The Bible As Story

Because the Bible is literature, it is not surprising that a goodly part of it is *story*. This fact carries an implication. At its simplest it means that story must be respected as story —one must accept its rules and conventions. One must enter into the story and move within it. If, for instance, one were to object that mice do not turn into horses nor a pumpkin into a carriage — only to change back again on the stroke of midnight — the story of Cinderella appears to be discredited. The objection may seem eminently 'sensible' and quite level-headed. Instead, it is wrong-headed, because it misses the whole point of *story*. Such misunderstanding has, too often, bedevilled the approach to biblical stories. Many have, for example, stumbled over that famous 'whale' of Jonah — and have got no further! For one who reads Jonah as story that 'great fish' is spontaneously seen for what it is, a clever device of the story-teller. Let us look at a few of those biblical stories.

1. Samson (Judges 13-16).

The Book of Judges, as edited by the Deuteronomists, is, like the rest of the Deuteronomical History, addressed to the Babylonian Exiles to explain the disaster of the Exile and to point to a future of hope. The varied stories of the 'judges' (local charismatic heroes) illustrate a recurring cycle of infidelity-punishment-repentance-deliverance. The stories themselves can be as different as that of Deborah and Barak (Jg 4-5), based on an historical encounter between Israelites and Canaanites, and the rambunctious folk-tale of Samson (Jg 13-16), but the pattern remains the same. And, while respecting the editorial intent, we should enjoy Samson for the earthy story it is. The editors did obviously appreciate it because, framework apart, they have presented it untouched.

Samson, a child of promise, was a 'nazir' — the sign of his dedication to God being his long hair which must never be cut. Endowed with immense strength, he carried on a one-man war against the Philistines. A recognizable story-feature is that of the invincible warrior vulnerable to every pretty face and figure. Samson's romantic encounters carry the story. On his way to the Philistine town of Timnah to visit his future wife, he killed a lion with his bare hands. A swarm of bees nesting in the vulture-picked skeleton provided the stuff of a riddle for his wedding-guests:

> Out of the eater came something to eat;
> out of the strong came something sweet (Jg 14:14).

The answer was prised from him by his wife (v.18) — a presage of future disaster.

Samson's exploits against the Philistines lose nothing in the telling. Not content with just simply setting a match to the harvest-dry standing grain of the enemy, our hero first caught three hundred foxes and used them as his arsonists —with flaming torches attached to the tied-together tails of each pair. Another time, he slew a thousand Philistines with the jawbone of an ass as his only weapon. Then he met Delilah! She wormed from him his secret: the source of his strength lay in the uncut seven locks of his hair — and a blinded Samson ground corn in a prison mill at Gaza. His shorn locks grew again and his strength flowed back. In the temple of Dagon he wreaked his vengeance: 'So the dead whom he slew at his death were more than those whom he had slain during his life' (16:30). A brilliant ending!

To savour this clever narrative, one must take the episode of the foxes in one's stride, must not ask why Samson, in the light of his previous experience, would have yielded to Delilah's tactic, nor wonder why the Philistines could have overlooked the fact that his shorn locks were growing again... One does not put such questions to *story*.

2. David and Bathsheba (2 Samuel 11-12).

The finest bit of prose in the Old Testament is the so-called 'Succession Narrative' of 2 Sam 9 — 1 Kgs 2 — the history of the family of David and of the struggle for succession to his throne. The complex character of David is sharply etched in the superb story of his encounter with Bathsheba. He had caught sight of the woman as she bathed and must have his way with her — though she was the wife of another. It is clear that this adultery was an open secret; the husband Uriah was quite aware that he had been cuckolded (11:1-13). David, in an attempted cover-up, engineered the death of Uriah (11:12-13). It was cold-blooded murder. The only redeeming feature is that, when challenged by a prophet, David acknowledged his double sin (12:1-15). He made no excuses. The sequel shows him free once more of his disastrous aberration and measuring up to his true stature.

This we see in the vivid closing narrative: David's prayer for his stricken child, the child of his adultery (12:15-23). He fasted and prayed while the sick child lived; on hearing of the infant's death, he made no mourning. And he explained his unusual conduct: 'While the child was still alive, I fasted and wept, for I said, "Who knows whether the Lord will be gracious to me, that the child may live?" But now he is dead; why should I fast? Can I bring him back again?' (12:22-23). It is David's finest hour.

David had confessed and repented, but he had sown his dragons' teeth; he must reap the harvest of bitter family strife. The great king turns out to be a comforting biblical hero: for all his greatness he is flesh and blood and has his times of weakness and failure. We can see him so because we see him through the eyes of a gifted story-teller. But only if we really listen to the story will we meet this David in whom we may glimpse something of ourselves.

3. Jonah.

Despite the glowing poetic promise of Second Isaiah (Is 40-55) return from the Babylonian Exile was on a depressingly small scale. In the tiny Jewish state of the fifth century the struggle to preserve national identity was painful. It is understandable that, among the returned exiles and their descendants, in view of all they had been through and were still suffering, a certain exclusiveness, a ghetto-mentality, should have appeared — at least in some circles. Those who shared this outlook wished to cut themselves off from contact with other peoples and looked with impatience for the vengeance of God on the Gentiles. Jonah is a criticism of this stance and a bold declaration that God is the God of all peoples. It is no naive collection of improbable miracles but is a highly-sophisticated writing, a brilliant satire.

Jonah is presented as a prophet of the Chosen People, one entrusted with a divine mission. This mission is to preach to the Assyrians, the hated oppressors of his people. The prophet well knew the mercy of God and he suspected that, in fact, the Assyrians would repent and God would not carry out his threat against them. The thought of the divine mercy extended to the great enemy was more than Jonah could stand. Hence, instead of setting out for Nineveh, in the east, he fled to the west (Jon 1:1-3). The famous 'great fish' of Jon 1:17; 2:10 is no more than an 'executive submarine' to get Jonah back on the job!

With splended artistry the author contrasts the narrow, unforgiving disposition of the Israelite prophet with the open and sympathetic attitude of the other actors in his story — all Gentiles. The pagan sailors are horrified to learn that anyone can bring himself to disobey a divine command (1:10) and they are loath to cast him into the sea. The king of Nineveh and his people at once believe the word of the prophet and are converted and do penance (3:6-9). The irony is unmistakable: the preaching of the reluctant Jonah meets with an immediate and universal response in the pagan city, whereas the great prophets had, over the centuries, preached to the Chosen People in vain!

God did accept the sincere conversion of the Ninevites; but what of Jonah? 'It displesed Jonah exceedingly and he was angry' (4:1). But he did not give up hope that the Lord might yet change his mind, and sat outside the city, waiting for the desired destruction (4:5). Then God, who was all patience and mercy even towards his stubborn prophet, taught him a lesson in a gentle but effective way. He caused a plant to spring up and give shelter to Jonah, and then he permitted it to wither just as quickly — to the chagrin of the prophet (4:6-9). The moral of the story is made clear: If Jonah felt that he had a right to be annoyed because the plant had withered up, should not God pity Nineveh in which were more than 120,000 helpless infants ('who do not know their right hand from their left' (4:11), as well as many animals, and not seek to destroy it? The loving mercy of God extends to all peoples and to all his creatures.

205

The 'big fish' should never have figured as *the* problem of Jonah. Much more striking is the fantastic dimensions given to the city: 'Nineveh was an exceedingly great city, three days' journey in breadth' (3:3); Jonah felt that he had not really arrived in the city until he had walked for a whole day across it! (3:4). The immense number of infants noted would suit the population of such a megapolis. Most remarkable of all is the conversion of king and people. It is formally stated that the people of Nineveh believed God (3:5) and God himself acknowledged the sincerity of their conversion (3:10).

The literal-minded will question the 'fish,' will challenge, on archaeological grounds, the size and population of Nineveh and, on historical grounds, the conversion of the Assyrians. One who listens to story will take all in his stride. For he will see in it the God who is caring Father of all — and hear in it a stark challenge. The challenge is that of Jesus himself: 'Love your enemy!' *Story* is dangerous. We are adept at pulling its teeth.

4. Tobit.

The book of Tobit is concerned with a double case of the just sufferer. Tobit, meticulous in religious observance and magnanimous in his charity — the model Jew in short — is the victim of an unfortunate accident. Sarah, an innocent girl, is grievously afflicted through no fault of her own. Both become the butt of bitter tongues (2:14; 3:8) and, as a result, both seek to die (3:7,15). The key to the book is found in 3:16-17 and 12:12-15. The prayer of the two unhappy ones is presented to God by Raphael and the angel is entrusted with a mission to help them. The portrait of Azarias (the angel Raphael in human form) is based on Gen 24:40 — 'He (Abraham) said to me: "The Lord before whom I walk, will

206

send his angel with you to prosper your way; and you shall take a wife for my son from my kindred." ' Azarias is indeed an instrument of God's providence; he is a dramatic answer to prayer.

The modern reader will feel at home with this writing: it is a novel. The stories of Tobit and Sarah come together at 3:16-17 — their separate prayers had met in the presence of God. With superb skill, the author traces the manner of God's response. Tobit (4:1) recalled that he had, years before, entrusted a sum of money to his friend Gabael and he now decided to send his son Tobias to claim it. To be his son's companion and guide on the journey he hired a Jew named Azarias (the reader knows that he is, in fact, the angel Raphael). The angel encouraged the young man in face of danger and aided him to procure a remedy for his father's blindness and also one against the machinations of evil spirits — thus he could deliver Sarah (6:1-8). Moreover, he so effectively extolled the charms of Sarah that Tobias, before ever he had set eyes on the girl, 'fell in love with her and lost his heart to her hopelessly' (6:17). At Ecbatana they visited the home of Raguel. Tobias wasted no time in seeking Sarah's hand. And the story then moves towards its 'they lived happily ever after' ending.

The reader has to go along with the story-teller in the 'angel in human form' theme and must accept the jealous love of the demon Asmodeus for the beautiful Sarah. There is another 'great fish' — this one with vital parts that can get rid of demons and cure blindness. And one must believe that Tobit could have completely forgotten about a large sum of money he had, years before, given to a friend in trust — especially at a time when he needed money badly. Perhaps the one touch that will not surprise is that of the level-headed Raguel digging a grave by night (8:9) lest Tobias should go the way of his seven unfortunate predecessors! For the one who enters into the spirit of the story its meaning becomes clear and its challenge unmistakable.

5. The Prodigal Son (Luke 15:11-32).

Jesus was a consummate story-teller. It is not surprising that his parables are the most widely-known parts of the New Testament. A parable is a special kind of story: a story, always of an ethical or religious bent, that has two levels of meaning; it has much more to it than meets the eye. Below the surface lurks a depth of meaning and a challenge. Let us see a striking example.

'There was a man who had two sons' — so opens the familiar parable of The Prodigal Son. Its Lucan setting would fix it, readily, in the ministry of Jesus: 'The pharisees and the scribes murmured, saying, "This man rceives sinners and eats with them."' (Lk 15:2). Jesus' parable is a defence of his own conduct, his concern for the 'little ones' whom the pharisees had written off as outcasts. Defence, yes — but profoundly challenging.

Jesus' Jewish hearers would have grasped the pathos of the young man's plight: a Jew herding pigs! — he had struck rock-bottom. What they would have found disconcerting was the incredible conduct of the father. To receive back without word of reproof and without any condition at all one who had shown himself so weak, was unbelievably foolish. They would have identified, readily, with the hard-headed other son. The fact that the story itself manifestly extols the conduct of the father would have given pause. What is it all about?

Jesus would suggest that the weakness of the younger son is *vulnerability*. He is vulnerable both to his fair-weather friends and to the love of his father. The rectitude of the elder son is effective armour against the plea of vulnerability and the foolishness of love. He had never really known his father and he now rejects his brother who had besmirched the family name. Had he not a point? To receive back, without sanctions, one who had already proved fickle, was rash in the extreme. It was crass favouritism — this cosseting of a profligate and neglect of one who had always served and obeyed!

This is a disturbing story, on many counts — a disturbing story for us Christians of today. Already, Luke has taken it out of the ministry of Jesus and addressed it directly to the 'pharisees' of his own community. And surely we must look to ourselves, to our own possible resentment at God's graciousness to sinners. We can find comfort in the warm treatment of the younger son. Always there is the father. He is the real challenge. For this story of the father and his two sons is allegory; the characters are God, the sinner and the righteous. The gracious, forgiving Father holds the stage.

What does this powerful story say to me? It speaks, eloquently, of a loving God's concern for humankind, in particular of his 'favouritism' of the outcast. It sets a question-mark against the theology of forgiveness of sin reflected in so much of our penitential practice. God's forgiveness is just too good to be true. Above all there is the uncomfortable truth that one can really get to know this Father *only* by acknowledging the brother and sister as brother and sister. It is dangerous to listen to this kind of story.

6. Jesus and the Samaritan Woman (John 4).

Jesus the story-teller was also the inspirer of stories, as the gospels show. We have, for instance, the encounter of Jesus with the Samaritan woman at Jacob's well. A weary Jesus sat by a well in hostile Samaria. 'How is it that you, a Jew, ask a drink of me, a woman of Samaria?' (Jn 4:9) — a world of meaning packed into a single question. Why this breach of convention that a man should so casually address a lone woman? The disciples, later, could not hide their scandal at such conduct: 'they marveled that he was talking with a woman' (v.27). And, a Jew ought to know better than ask a favour of a Samaritan! But the woman had spoken in reply and a dialogue was afoot.

Jesus introduced the theme of 'living water' and caught her interest; she is soon thirsting for the water of life. When Jesus displays an embarrassing insight into her private life one sympathizes with the woman's hasty change of subject: Where is true cult to be offered to God (vv 20-24). And, convinced that she has met the Messiah, she hastened to spread the news — leaving her water jar behind! (v.28). The Samaritans, impressed by her story, came to meet Jesus and then, having met him, become patronising towards her (v.42).

The narrative is the story of a coming to faith. Notable is the list of titles bestowed on Jesus. At first he is 'a Jew' (v.9) then, more respectfully, 'Sir' (v.11). The suspicion that he may be 'greater than our father Jacob' (v.12) introduces a new note. Rapidly, he is a 'prophet' (v.19) and, finally, 'the Christ' (v.29). The climax comes with the Samaritans' observation that though the woman's testimony was what first led them to Jesus, when they met him all else faded into the background: 'we have heard for ourselves and we know that this is indeed the Saviour of the world' (v.42). The story closes on this glorious title.

We can identify with the woman. We need to grow in our understanding of Jesus. To let him into our lives can be embarrassing; his light shows up what is within us, lighting areas we would rather leave in the dark. Above all, we learn that we know him by personal encounter and that we can have from him the water of life.

7. The Passion Stories.

As, each year, we enter Lent and glimpse Holy Week on the horizon, we are reminded, rather more sharply, of the passion and death of Jesus. We may have thought that we possess, in our gospels, a straightforward account of what took place. There are, of course, some discrepancies in the four versions but, on the whole, we know how it was. Today, with a better appreciation of the role of an evangelist, we recognize four distinct presentations of the passion story, each one filtered through decades of christian faith-experience and growth in christological thought. A comparison of even two of the passion narratives will help us to realize that truth is so much larger than any human expression of it. A detailed comparative study of the passion narratives of Mark (14:1 — 15:39) and John (chs 18-19) is outside our scope. It will be enough to look at the arrest stories and end with a more general observation.

In Mk 14:43-50 Judas plays a leading role. He led the arresting party sent by 'the chief priests and the scribes and the elders' to the place where Jesus and the others were. He took care to identify Jesus by greeting him with a disciple's kiss; and the arrest was made. Jesus was passive. His only protest was at the manner of the arrest: they had come, armed, to take a man of violence. But he was a man of peace who had nothing to hide. At that point 'they all forsook him, and fled' — he was abandoned by his disciples.

John's account (18:1-11) is very different. Judas does lead 'a band of soldiers' to the right place — but remains firmly in the background. Jesus takes the initiative and strides forward to confront the group: 'Whom do you seek?'

At his 'I AM' (the divine name) 'they drew back and fell to the ground.' He permits himself to be taken — but on his conditions: 'let these men go.' The disciples do not desert him — he defends them. He is wholly master of the situation.

It is impossible to reconcile the accounts in terms of what really happened. There is little doubt that the arrest would have been much as Mark tells it. But one must be aware, too, that the narrative fits Mark's purpose of showing a Jesus 'delivered up' and abandoned by all, who will die utterly forsaken (15:34-37). For Mark the cross is the only true sign of who Jesus really is — that is the point of the centurion's profession of faith: 'Truly, this man was Son of God' (15:39). His whole passion narrative (indeed his whole gospel) is designed to show that only one who, like that centurion, can accept the paradox of the cross can know and confess Jesus the Christ.

John presents the passion as the triumph of the Son of God. It closes on a cry of victory: 'It is fulfilled' (19:30). Jesus had chosen the moment of death (v.28). He had been in command all along — witness the appearance before Pilate (18:28 — 19:16). The arrest narrative is wholly consistent with the rest of the Johannine passion-story.

Yet again we have to listen to the story-tellers and enter their world. The differences we have noted at the start of these stories continue throughout. The difference is stark at the end — the accounts of the crucifixion (Mk 15:21-39; Jn 19:17-37). The Marcan Jesus dies, helplessly, in awful isolation — his life crushed from him. The Johannine Jesus dies, in his own good time, with a cry of triumph on his lips. For Mark death reveals the Sonship of Jesus; for John the death is the glorification of the Son of God.

Obviously, there is much in common here — because Mark and John share the same *faith*. But they do not share

212

the same *theology*. For John, Jesus is the Word-made-flesh. His christology is incarnational: Jesus is the pre-existing Word incarnate. Mark's christology is *not* incarnational; he knows nothing of a pre-existing Word. But his Jesus, as firmly as John's, is Son of God. Our christology would be immeasurably poorer if we lacked either Mark or John. Jesus' cruel death on the cross plumbed the depths of human pain and isolation. The Jesus who died was Son of God and source of life. To appreciate the richness we need to listen to both Mark *and* John.

8. The Road to Emmaus (Lk 24:13-35).

In his closing story of the risen Lord and the two disciples on the road to Emmaus, Luke has, in his own way, taken the resurrection of Jesus out of the past and brought it into our present. It is more than a story — it is a sophisticated eucharistic catechesis: a 'liturgy of the word' followed by a 'liturgy of the eucharist.' The conversation between Jesus and the two disciples, in which they discuss recent events and he answers them, is a clear outline of the primitive preaching in Acts. Jesus lived, died and was raised from the dead, a fact that is witnessed in the scriptures and proved by the testimony of the apostles.

Yet, it is an enthralling story. The description of the situation of the two disciples is poignant. They had been impressed by Jesus; they had hoped for a divine intervention while he was still alive; but their hopes had been shattered by his death. They had obviously remained firmly tied to Jewish messianic expectation. But after Jesus had explained *all* that the scriptures taught about the coming Messiah, they gained a deep insight into the revelation of God that is Christ. In the plan of God the cross was the necessary road to glory. There is a lot of ourselves in the two disciples. The

213

ragged story of our life reveals its full splendour only when viewed in the context of Christ.

Yet the disciples did not really recognise Jesus until the 'breaking of the bread.' Luke's readers could not have missed his point. Not alone was 'the breaking of the bread' already a familiar designation of the eucharist, the terms describing the action of Jesus at table — he *took ... blessed ... broke ... gave* (v.30) — are consciously eucharistic language (cf 22:19). Luke is telling us here that in the eucharist we experience a meeting with Christ. We share a meal with Jesus in which he gives himself to us. The risen Jesus is encountered when and wherever the church 'breaks bread.' And Luke has made his theological statement on the presence of the Lord in word and sacrament through the challenging form of story.

Chapter Eleven
Why Read The Bible?

If we have been moderately successful in conveying some sense of the worth and the flavor of the Bible, we will already have gone a long way towards answering the question: *Why read the Bible?* The real reason why we should read it is because it is word of God, his gift to us. We have sought to explain what 'word of God' means. We have insisted that this status detracts not at all from the human qualities and limitations of the writings. Not all of the Bible is easy going, not all of it makes inspiring reading. But we are meant to enjoy it when and where we can, and there is much that is charming and refreshing.

A. For Our Salvation

The Bible might be approached as a fascinating, and an important, human achievement. In prose and poetry it contains much that ranks with the best of the world's literature. When one considers the political and economical insignificance of Israel it is a matter for wonder that we know as much as we do about this people. The New Testament is more remarkable still. Here we have not the record of a tenacious people but the story of one man and his incredible impact on those who followed him. Jesus of Nazareth was a Palestinian Jew, living in a turbulent but out-of-the-way corner of the Roman Empire. He ran foul of the Jewish religious authorities who plotted to get rid of him. They were able to prevail on a petty Roman administrator and Jesus was duly executed. Not surprisingly, the whole sordid episode raised not a ripple in the mainstream Roman world. The situation became serious when, convinced that this crucified Jesus had risen from the dead, his followers began to win adherents throughout that world. On the whole, though, this 'christian' movement appeared to be either some variety of Judaism or another oriental sect. At this early stage the movement did not seem to have much of a future. We may be sure that, outside of christian circles, the books of the New Testament were virtually unknown.

The wonder is that these books of the Old Testament and these writings of the New are still with us. Surprisingly, the Old Testament is not only of interest to the descendants of the people who brought it into being. It remains part of the Scripture of all christian Churches and its impact, over the centuries, has been enormous. And that insignificant christian movement did not fizzle out but grew into a worldwide religion, one which has molded the civilization of the western world. The New Testament has proved to be the most influential literature in history. The Bible is still very much part of our world.

A meeting-place

Just because the Bible has been so influential, it has also been made an occasion or a means of discord. It is surely an oversimplification to declare that the Protestant Reformation was based solely on an interpretation of Paul's doctrine of justification. But it is sadly true that his letter to the Romans

216

did become a weapon, wielded bludgeon-like, by Catholic and Protestant. And it is true also that, because of Protestant proprietary claims over the Bible, the Roman Church, to its own loss, in practice depreciated Scripture. Happily, in our day, Roman Catholics have re-discovered the Bible. And, in a healthier atmosphere of ecumenism, it has become a meeting-place and a bond. It is noteworthy that when, a few years ago, a group of French scholars, of different denominations, launched an ecumenical translation of the Bible, they deliberately began with Romans. This sign of contradiction had become a challenge to christian peace and brotherhood, and they boldly and successfully faced the challenge. For the Church of today the Bible has become more and not less important.

Word of God

This should not surprise us. As believers we take the Bible to be word of God. Inspired by his Spirit, it is surely sustained by the Spirit. There is always the hazard that we acknowledge all this to be so, and do nothing about it: a familiar human trait. It may not be going too far to say that a mark of the seriousness of our christian commitment is our concern with the Bible. If we are convinced that it is word of God, we will want to know more about it. If we regard it as indeed God's gift to us, we will want to respond to his gracious giving. An adequate response is not in the purchase of a handsomely-bound, illustrated Bible to grace a coffee table. We will want to read and ponder this word of God. For he has spoken to us for our salvation.

We should recognize that God's speaking to us in our terms is not condescension but courtesy. He wants to put us at our ease. Above all, he wants to communicate. He has spoken to us by people like ourselves. We can identify with

217

the personages of the Bible because all of them are flesh and blood. They are nobly or ignobly human; the Bible is happily free of the unlikely saints of later hagiography. But by God's supreme gesture of courtesy, we can identify with the Word-made-flesh, for he had become 'like his brethren in every respect' (Heb 2:17). We read the Bible to know our Father and to hear his word. We read in order to hear the words of eternal life spoken by the Son. We read to learn the way of godly living and to find comfort and encouragement on the way. God has taken the trouble (to put it like that) to provide this reading matter for us. Surely we, literate Christians, might be expected to show some appreciation of the fact. And there is only one practical manner of showing appreciation: to take and read. The fact that the Bible is not easy reading should be a challenge, not a deterrent. Besides, we can exaggerate the difficulties. We shall try to show, in a final chapter, that, in some measure, we can have 'Scripture without tears'.

B. The God of the Bible

Not long ago, the 'death of God' was in vogue. One could hope that, in some respects, God were really dead. I mean, for instance, that venerable white-haired figure seated benignly on a cloud. One would also hope that another God is dead: the tyrannical God of fear — the 'God of the Old Testament'. And surely one would hope that this God is dead: that faceless, bloodless 'providence' that is vaguely 'there'. In short, one would wish that all human 'Gods' were dead and buried. The real God of the Bible is something other. Perhaps, deep down, our reluctance to read the Bible has something of that discomfiture of fallen man and woman in the garden (Gen 3:8-10): we are afraid to come face to face with this God. Or, it may be that we fear what may be asked of us. To encounter God: that is a chastening thought. And it will happen if we approach his word in the openness and humility of believing. But need we be afraid?

One can find in Scripture a text to support any view, no matter how crazy. Politicians know too well how, by selective quotation, they can be made to say the opposite of what they had really said. To quote a text without reference to the immediate and broader context, can be travesty. We have drawn attention to the inevitability of theological development over the long period covered by the Old Testament. And, because we are dealing with real-life human affairs, we are bound to find traces of primitive theological views.

A God of fear?

We can, without much difficulty, find support for this fearsome 'God of the Old Testament'. He is bloodthirsty. Look at chapters 10 and 11 of Joshua. In two campaigns, Joshua put all the Canaanite inhabitants of the land to the sword — 'because the Lord God of Israel fought for Israel'. Then turn to Judges to find that Joshua's 'final solution' had flopped: those 'slain' Canaanites were a mortal danger to Israel. There are two factors here. The early Israelites accepted the principle of 'holy war' current in their Semitic world. A feature of this was that a whole village would be designated for extinction — as an offering to the god. Yahweh *never* commanded the destruction of a town or a people; but, at an early stage, Israel did so interpret his will. Then, chapters 10-11 of Joshua are wholly the work of the deuteronomical editors and are a 'theological' presentation of the Conquest which makes no claim (witness the rest of the book) to be historically accurate. Joshua's bloodbath never happened.

219

An arbitrary God?

A disturbing instance of the arbitrariness of God appears in 2 Samuel 6. David had decided to bring the ark (dwelling-place of Yahweh and sign of his presence) back from former Philistine territory. It was solemnly installed on a new ox-cart and was conveyed with pomp and ceremony. All went well until the oxen stumbled and the ark seemed in danger of toppling. A certain Uzzah sought to prevent that calamity — and was rewarded for his solicitude! 'Uzzah put out his hand to the ark of God and took hold of it, for the oxen stumbled. And the anger of the Lord was kindled against Uzzah; and God smote him there because he put forth his hand to the ark; and he died there beside the ark of God' (2 Sam 6:6-7). The story surely represents a primitive, magical, view of the 'holiness' of the ark. Inconsistently, those who dared to load the ark got away with it — only poor, simple Uzzah was stricken.

It surely must be that the rare instances of the 'arbitrariness' and 'bloodthirstiness' of God should be set in context. And in that broader setting he appears in very different light. The God of Hosea is a husband who agonizes over his unfaithful wife, who will not give her up. He is the Father who bends down to feed his infant child. Jeremiah can boldly tell his God that his demands on him are unreasonable. The psalmists unashamedly put their needs before an understanding God. The prayers in Daniel, Ezra, and Nehemiah are addressed to a benevolent God. In short, this travesty-figure, the 'God of the Old Testament', springs from ignorance of, or gross misunderstanding of, the Old Testament.

Our Father

Who, then, is God? Our God is the Father of our Lord Jesus Christ, who has shown himself in the life and cross of Jesus. He is truly the God of the Old Testament, whom Jesus knew and addressed as 'Father'. The difference is that, through the revelation of the Son, *we* see him more clearly. The New Testament brings more sharply and emphatically before us a concerned and caring Father: 'God so loved the world that he gave his only Son' (Jn 3:16). Our God is the Father who has given us his Son — given us himself. We measure love by our experience of love. We have to measure even the divine love by our human standards. Only in heaven shall we know what love is — God's love for us. Here we need to think the unthinkable, believe the unbelievable. God does love us so much that he has given us his Son, and given himself in the gift. We are Christians, followers of Christ. We must, always, take the Incarnation with the utmost seriousness. God has revealed himself to us in the human figure, in the life, death, and resurrection of Jesus Christ. In him God has come to walk among us. But he is always the same God, the one God, who speaks to us from the first page of the Bible to the last.

C. The Man and Woman of the Bible

The Bible does not deal in stained-glass saints. Its men and women are robust and full-blooded: saints and sinners and a mixture of both. For the most part we meet believers. There are some exceptions. It is hard to pin down Ahab. But there is no doubt concerning his wife Jezebel: she is a militant worshiper of Baal. While the religion of Yahweh was in a sorry mess during the long reign of Manasseh, it is hard to

221

know to what extent the king was a helpless victim of political circumstances. We might add to the list, but the people who interest us most are those whose faith in God had to be lived and maintained in their own humanness and in the midst of life's reality. It was never easy, and sometimes extraordinarily difficult for them to persevere and mature. They turn out to be people very like ourselves, sharing our frailty and our fears. The difference, very often, is found in their openness and generosity and courage.

How to be human

Above, we have seen something of Jeremiah and Ezekiel, of the author of Job and of Qoheleth. In the New Testament Paul stands out. Above all, God, in Jesus, has shown us what true humanness is. He has shown us that 'nothing is so strong as gentleness; nothing is so gentle as real strength'. He has radically challenged our values. Far more importantly, he gives us the means to be ourselves, to be fully human. We need to listen to him and to learn. We need to discover something of the flame that lit the hearts of the disciples of Emmaus (Lk 24:32). We need to look to those who were transformed by his word.

Woman

We have spoken of the human conditioning of the Bible. Nowhere is this more evident than in its attitude to women. The Bible reflects a man's world. It is inevitable that it should do so, given the male-dominated culture in which it emerged. There is no doubt, for instance, that the wisdom writers show a markedly misogynistic strain. Against this background a recognition of the true status of woman, discreet

222

though it may be, but unmistakable, is all the more significant. We have noted the position taken in Genesis 1-2 where
woman's equality with man is acknowledged. It is equality
and not competition. She finds fulfillment as woman and
not otherwise.

In the New Testament the situation has changed —
more radically than, perhaps, we realize. Quite surprising
is the number of episodes in the gospels which concern
women and their meetings with Jesus. The courteous Luke,
especially, has related his Lord's gentle sensitivity towards
them. Women were Jesus' friends, and he ignored the contemporary custom of keeping them in inferior seclusion.
There were the women disciples who followed him and
ministered to him (Lk 8:1-3). Although her identity is unknown, there is the woman who anointed him out of her
abundant love (Lk 7:36-50). His healing of the woman with
a hemorrhage is symbolic of his understanding of all the
needs of womanhood (Mk 5:25-34). Above all, he stepped
right into their lives where social custom would have for-
bidden it. He forgave the woman accused of adultery because
his gentle, merciful eyes saw beyond her frailty, and because
he cut clean across a male double-standard (Jn 8:1-11). And,
where a rabbi would not speak even with his own wife in
public, Jesus conversed freely with the Samaritan woman —
to the evident scandal of his disciples (Jn 4:27). And there
is the eloquent statement of John: 'Now Jesus *loved* Martha
and her sister Mary . . .' (11:5). Simply, women were Jesus'
friends. What more courteous way of restoring women to
their proper place in God's plan.

Champion of women

Here, as always, Paul is the faithful disciple. The misogynism of the sages is an established fact; the alleged

misogynism of Paul is calumny. After Jesus none better than he has struck a blow for women. It is significant that a call for the submissive obedience of women is found only in the suspect letters (most likely Paul never wrote them) to the Colossians and Ephesians and especially in 1 Timothy. It is revealing to compare 1 Cor 11:2-16 with 1 Tim 2:11-12. In the one Paul struggles to find some reason to persuade the women of the non-Jewish community of Corinth to wear a fitting head-dress at the christian assemblies; their practice of going bare-headed had offended his Jewish susceptibility. (It has been argued, plausibly, that what is involved is a 'unisex' hairstyle!) It is amusing to see Paul make such heavy weather of this 'problem'; one smiles, at the end, at his exasperated 'it is not the custom.' How very different the approach of his disciple in 1 Tim 2:12 — 'I permit no woman to teach or to have authority over men; she is to remain silent.' There is the voice of petty ecclesiastical authority. Paul was too big a man to command women to wear hats; this lesser ecclesiastic arrogantly reduced them to silence.

It is not Paul but this wholly un-Pauline arrogance that women should blame for their present status as second-class citizens in the Church. Paul it was who made the astounding statement: 'There is . . . neither male nor female, for you are all one in Christ Jesus' name (Gal 3:28). As a Christian, woman is wholly the equal of man. It is a return to God's plan of creation, achieved by Christ. And Paul followed it through in practice. We read of a host of women whom Paul acknowledged to be in the service of the gospel: Priscilla (Acts 15:2), Lydia (16:14), Chloe (1 Cor 1:11), Phoebe (Rom 16:1) — to name but a few. Women have a right to point across the centuries to the example and teaching of the Lord and of Paul. That they should discover and vindicate their rightful place in the Body of Christ would be a very welcome fruit of the reading of the Bible. There is no place for second-class citizens in the household of the Lord.

Why read the Bible? We have been trying all along, to answer that question. Perhaps, in some respect, the answer is the same as that to the question: why climb a mountain? Because it is there. The Bible is our 'mountain' which Christians are called to climb. Both Paul and the author of Hebrews see Christian life as a race to be run, so our metaphor is not too far-fetched. For us Christians the Bible is there, word of God. It is a 'mountain' to be faced with resolution and perseverance. And we will grow weary. But from the summit we shall view the Promised Land. On that summit we can breathe fresh, invigorating air. And in that smogless light we can see our religion in fresh focus. And we can glimpse the christian way stretching out as a challenge — not meandering aimlessly but leading to a goal: the lasting city of God (Heb 13:14).

Chapter Twelve

How To Read The Bible

We have been looking closely at the Bible. We have seen how it is word of God; and we have sampled it. We have outlined its contents and given an impression of its literary quality and religious worth. And we have advanced some reasons why we should read and study it. Now it is fitting that we should offer some advice on how to set about reading and studying the Bible. In this closing chapter, in view of what has gone before, we can revert to the normal procedure and take the Old Testament first.

A. The Heart of the Old Testament

In chapter two we offered a selection of passages from the Old Testament. The purpose of the sample was to introduce the reader as gently as possible to the Old Testament, to help one get the feel of it. Now it is time for something more ambitious. We propose a selection that should reveal the heart of the Old Testament. It might seem preposterous to seek to catch the essence of the Old Testament in what, for practical purposes, must be a short reading-list. But one must make the attempt if the reader is to be helped. We do not at all suggest that one may concentrate on those writings

226

and safely ignore the rest. Far from it. If this book has at all achieved its purpose it should have encouraged one to read and study the *Bible*. An initial selective reading program is calculated to provide just such encouragement.

1. EXODUS

In some sense the Exodus is the Old Testament equivalent of the Incarnation: it is the mighty intervention of God. Already the exodus episode has taken on an epic quality. More importantly, it has become a theological event: the assurance to Israel of its call and of the presence of its God. The faith of the Old Testament is founded on the Exodus-event.

2. AMOS

Though listed among the 'minor prophets' Amos is, by any standard, a major figure. In a sense he is the prototype of a prophet. He stands forth as a fearless vindicator of right. And his passion for social justice makes him a prophet of our time.

3. DEUTERONOMY

Even the legislative sections (Chapters 12-26) should be read because of their distinctive flavor. But the three discourses of Moses are truly moving, especially when one knows their historical setting (see chapter eight above). This is the book of the Old Testament closest in spirit to the New Testament. It is no surprise that it is quoted there so freely.

4. SECOND ISAIAH (Is 40-55)

The author of this powerful message of consolation had taken to heart the lesson of Deuteronomy. Here is the finest sustained literary product of the prophetic movement. And it introduces the evocative figure of the Suffering Servant of Yahweh.

5. THE BOOK OF JOB

This magnificent poem certainly deserves its place in any short list of Old Testament writings. In chapter eight above one will find a sketch of its argument and an impression of its worth. One might, surreptitiously, slip in the book of Qoheleth. While complementary to Job it is a masterpiece in its own right.

6. 2 CHRONICLES

This might seem a surprising choice. But it is important to grasp the Hebrew understanding of history. The Chronicler has given us a theology of history. He can consciously adapt and embellish the details of his source (Kings) in order to make his theological point. The procedure of the evangelists is not very different.

7. THE BOOK OF WISDOM

Included not primarily because it is the latest Old Testament writing. As an example of the wisdom literature it can be surprisingly modern (see, for instance, the 'rationalism' of 2:1-5). Yet it is, in part, 'midrashic', with chapters 16-19 being a free reading of Exodus.

If, together with the writings listed here, one has read the passages indicated in chapter two, then one has read a goodly and representative portion of the Old Testament. It is then no longer a closed book. One hopes that it will remain an open and favorite book.

B. The Heart of the New Testament

It does seem easier to make a selection that might reasonably be said to represent the heart of the New Testament. Of course one has to be conscious of some subjectivity in the choice. What has been said about the non-exclusive nature of the Old Testament selection has equal validity here.

1. MARK

It is well to begin with a gospel. Mark's gospel, being the earliest, and the shortest, is a logical choice. Besides, in instancing Mark, a whole gospel without qualification, we wish to convey that each of the four gospels is to be seen as a distinctive work, complete in itself. A faulty approach, popular not so long ago, of offering a 'harmonized' text (a *Harmony of the Four Gospels*) is to be deprecated. Here, as for each of these selected readings, it would be well to look to the relevant introductory passage in our chapter three above.

2. ACTS OF THE APOSTLES

Acts, the work of Luke, is the sequel to his gospel. But it is not out of place after Mark, which offers essentially the same gospel-story. We are to recall the two main parts of Acts: chapters 1-15, the beginnings; and chapters 16-28, the spread of the gospel, a dramatic story centered in Paul.

A gospel and Acts — the foundation is laid. But it is well to keep in mind that both the one and the other have been written in the light of resurrection-faith. The gospel lets us glimpse the risen Lord. And Acts emphatically shows the power of the Spirit of the Lord behind the spread of the word.

3. 1 CORINTHIANS

Paul deals with a recalcitrant community. He had learned of divisions in the Corinthian church and of serious problems there. He patiently replies to a series of questions the Corinthians had submitted to him. We find a blend of pastoral concern and theological acumen. It is vintage Paul. The Pauline letters are never easy going but they are of the essence of the New Testament.

4. ROMANS

This is *the* Pauline letter. It would be unthinkable that a selection purporting to represent the 'heart of the New Testament' should not include it. Paul's gospel comes through: salvation offered to all, but through faith in Jesus Christ. In other words: salvation is a free gift and has taken concrete shape in God's offer of himself to us in Christ. It might seem like cheating to suggest that the reader should first take Galatians (slipping an extra into our short list). Because of its close relationship Galatians would be a helpful warmer-up for the more formidable Romans.

5. 1 JOHN

The epitome of christian spirituality. There is more here than meets the eye because of the deceptive simplicity of John's style. A spirituality that takes its stand on the Incarnation is surely well-grounded. And we are uncomfortably challenged to see and accept that love of God and love of neighbor are one. These five short chapters do indeed stand at the heart of the New Testament.

6. HEBREWS

It is hoped that the treatment of it in chapter five above will have alerted the reader to the importance of Hebrews. It is not all that easy to follow since it presupposes a good understanding of the Old Testament. But it firmly points to the centrality of Christ in the christian way of life. And it bids us look with confidence to a living high priest who is our gracious advocate.

7. JOHN

The heart-core of the New Testament. Or, to change the metaphor, its summit. Not for nothing did John become known as The Theologian. Simple language is the vehicle of a profound message. John has told us explicitly why he wrote: that you may go on believing that the man, Jesus of Nazareth, is the Messiah of Jewish expectation — that he is much more: the Son of God. His gospel was written that through faith in Christ we may find life in him.

We repeat: this 'heart of the New Testament' is not the whole. It is representative and gives the gist of the message. But there is much else, which ought not be neglected. It would be ludicrous to seem to imply that Matthew and Luke and Ephesians are of lesser importance because they do not figure in this selection. And so with the other writings not mentioned. We have written a *Guide*. It should be accepted as such. Once what has been recommended has been read and appreciated, the reading of the other books will be more fruitful.

C. The Old and the New

By now we have a reasonably comprehensive view of both the Old Testament and the New Testament. We must take note of a widely-shared concern to find a link between the Testaments, and to fit the Old Testament in a meaningful way into a christian context. It seems that, in this respect, the category promise/fulfillment is valid, indeed inescapable: the Old Testament holds promises which are fulfilled in the New. The Old Testament as a whole looks to a *future*, and the Christian finds that future in the New Testament. However, that which unites the testaments is a situation, a fact, rather than a method of expressing that unity or of bringing out the christian relevance of the Old Testament. The fact that it forms the necessary background to the New Testament, that it is necessary for a proper understanding of the New Testament, indicates that it has a real value of its own. It is a mistake to absorb it into a christian system, to seek to divert its whole meaning in a christian direction.

The drama

The Old Testament is the word of God, but it is incomplete; the New Testament is its necessary complement and its goal. The saving plan of God unfolds from the Old Testament to the New; the testaments represent, respectively, the first and the final act of the divine drama. The Christian will read the Old Testament under two aspects: he will see it, in its own historical context, as a record of God's dealing with men and of men's response to God; and he will see it as the first act of a drama whose denouement he knows. He will find Christ in it — but in promise, in type, and beneath the surface of the text. The Old Testament is meaningful for him as God's word, where God has spoken 'in many and various ways'. He will hear that older word more clearly because he has heard the new word that God has spoken in his Son. The Bible is the word of the one God. Christ is the link between the two parts of this word, the preparation and the fulfillment. He it is who opens the eyes of men to find God's deeper meaning in the earlier word. But that earlier word, because it is God's word, has a profound meaning of its own.

Parallels

Let us see if we might illustrate the relationship of the testaments and the broad unity of the Bible in terms of our reading program. The suggested pairings may prove to be helpful pointers.

EXODUS — MARK

Both writings tell of God's entry into history and of the formation of a people of God. And both are written from a standpoint of faith which has influenced the telling.

2 CHRONICLES — ACTS

Good examples of biblical historical writing. Basic historical facts are taken for granted but the dominant concern is with the religious dimension. Both writings share an optimism grounded in the power of God. The endings are notably optimistic. An exiled people is assured of restoration to Judah and of a new temple in Jerusalem. Paul, a prisoner in Rome, nevertheless preaches the word 'quite openly and unhindered'.

WISDOM — 1 CORINTHIANS

It is certain that Paul knew the Book of Wisdom — there are echoes of it in several of his writings. Paul speaks here of a wisdom taught by the Spirit. Indeed, God has made Christ Jesus 'our wisdom'. He is truly the Wisdom of God that the sages had glimpsed.

JOB — ROMANS

These have in common the problem of sin, though envisaged and handled very differently. Job challenges the existence of a necessary link between suffering and sin and receives an answer in darkness. Paul faces up to the fact of universal sin and finds a clear answer in God's free salvation through Christ.

SECOND ISAIAH — HEBREWS

These meet in their elevated and confident theology. The Suffering Servant finds his fulfillment in the High Priest who learned obedience in the school of suffering.

AMOS — 1 JOHN

They show a passion for true religion, for practical concern:

Take away from me the noise of your songs;
to the melody of your harps I will not listen.
But let justice roll down like waters,
and righteousness like an ever-flowing stream
(Amos 5:23-34).

Little children, let us not love in word or speech
but in deed and in truth (1 Jn 3:18).

Kindred spirits, and yet there is the vital difference, the *christian* difference:

God gave us eternal life, and this life is in his Son.
He who has the Son has life;
he who has not the Son has not life (5:11-12).

DEUTERONOMY — JOHN

The bond is in their distinctive styles. A passage of Deuteronomy stands out as sharply in the Pentateuch as a passage of John among the gospels. There is that and their penchant for noble discourse, of Moses and of Jesus. And therein is the difference: the prophet whom the Lord knew face to face — and the Word-made-flesh who alone knows the Father.

These parallels are not to be pushed too far. The selections were not made in view of any eventual pairing. However, if the unity of the Bible is a reality it surely must be found in what purports to be the heart of the Old and of the New. There is a unity, but a subtle one, a unity that should be understood in a realistic and elastic manner. All is word of God; but it is so as word of promise and as word of fulfillment. The Old, while having a meaning and a worth of its own still tends towards something beyond itself. And the New not only sheds light on the Old. It has struck its roots in the soil of the Old and has grown out of it. It is a new growth — firmly rooted in that past.